Finding Your Midpoint

LOCATING THE BALANCED POSITIONS FOR YOUR LIFE AND MINISTRY

Marc Buxton

Global Surge Press

Manila, Philippines

Marc Buxton/Global Surge Press
www.globalsurge.org
Book Layout ©2017 BookDesignTemplates.com
Cover Art: John Lester Limpin

Ordering Information:

Quantity sales. Special discounts are available on quantity purchases by churches, missionaries, associations, and others. For details, contact the publisher.

Finding Your Midpoint: Locating the Balanced Positions for Your Life and Ministry/ Marc Buxton. —1st ed.
ISBN 979-8-9864191-2-1

Dedicated to my Dad, Mark

One of the most balanced people I know

Contents

Satan always sends error into the world in pairs that are opposites. His great hope is that you will get so upset about one of his errors, that you'll react into the opposite one, and he's got you.

•

| *Clive Staples Lewis*

I've been interested in the idea of balance for quite some time. There are many areas where God calls us to have a balance in our lives– to not go to one extreme or the other – but to find the happy middle, the balance, the midpoint, the combination of the two poles.

I perhaps first became really intrigued with the concept of balance when I got married. Up until that point, it was just me. I was pretty easy to balance with myself as far as myself was concerned - my schedule and my priorities did not often conflict. But when I had a family – first a wife and then children – balance became an area of intrigue. I started thinking about how to maintain "work-life balance" and such things like that. I began learning about tools and tactics to use to help find the happy medium, while along the way learning that there is no perfect solution. If anyone claims to have perfect work-life balance they are either lying or ignorant. But, it *is* a battle that can be fought effectively, and so I began to fight it (and still am).

As I became tuned into the idea of balance, I began to notice other areas of life that balance played a large role in. In fact, I noticed so many areas and so many nuances that I began to think that there must be something more to it than coincidence. It was almost as if God had designed the world with balance in mind, or at least it seemed plausible. I began to realize that there were areas of needed balance all around me – I just had to engage them.

Even Solomon, *the* wisest man to ever live, touched on balance:

Do not be overly righteous,
Nor be overly wise;
Why should you destroy yourself?
Do not be overly wicked,
Nor be foolish;
Why should you die before your time?
It is good that you grasp this,
And also not remove your hand from the other;
For he who fears God will escape them all.
Ecclesiastes 7:16-18

There is balance in the world that God created and in our role in it. Yes, we have dominion over the earth to subdue and control it and use it for our good. But at the same time, we are to care for and protect the animal, plant, and human life around us and in our care – we have authority with boundaries, not a blank check to do as we please. Henry Morris said that finding this happy medium is to ideally find the "optimum balance between human needs on the one hand, and maintenance of the pristine ecology on the other".[1] Is it possible to have this perfect balance? Probably not in our fallen state. But is it worth striving for? A worthy goal? Absolutely. Balance.

Balance is a far-reaching concept. It touches many different areas of Christian life. It is seen in many different areas in our world – in nature, in global religions, in our relationships, and even within our own selves.

In Buddhism, the concept of The Middle Way is promoted. It is the idea of finding balance in all areas of life. Buddha likened it to playing a lute, with the strings not too tight or too loose. Could it be that Buddhists are pursuing a principle that God has set in the world – balance – and they are just pursuing it in the wrong ways under false pretenses? Could it be that what every person everywhere is really looking for is the balance that God designed us to live in, and has provided in Jesus Christ?

Hang on to your cowboy hats. We are about to find out.

Marc Buxton
Baguio City, Philippines 2024

---

[1] Henry M. Morris, Ph.D. 1991. The Bible, Creation, and Ecology. *Acts & Facts*. 20 (11).

CHAPTER 1

A Balanced View of Self

Have you ever heard statements like these?

I need to love myself before I can love others.
I am created in God's image, so I have worth and value.
I need to forgive myself first so I can find peace to forgive others.

These statements *sound* good. You may feel good saying them or hearing them said. Why, they may even sound biblical. But....they are not. They are the world's view of self and image.

God's view is much different. His take on this issue of *self* is that I *already* love myself, and that I will most naturally do what I think is in my best interests by default.

For no one ever hated his own flesh, but nourishes and cherishes it, just as the Lord *does* the church.
Ephesians 5:29

This verse says that no human being, at any-time, anywhere, has ever *truly* hated himself, but that instead we as human beings innately provide for ourselves and care for ourselves. In other words, I am *automatically* concerned about myself already.

Did you look in the mirror this morning after you woke up? Most likely you did. I did. Why? Because I love myself! I want *me* to look good – or at least as close as I can manage to get to that ideal. (side note: pre-teen boys don't count in this particular sociological study, as they generally don't care what they look like regardless of the situation. Ask me how I know).

Here's another experiential proof. When you cut your finger on something, what do you do? I mean a really serious cut. Go watch TV? Scroll social media? Go out and get something to eat? No! You stop and *take care* of the wound. No one has to tell you to do that. You just do it. Because you just care about yourself by default.

Another example: I can tell you from years of ministry experience that the hardest thing to do is to motivate and lead volunteers who are hungry and ready to eat. Why? Because if we are hungry, we are concerned about one thing – nourishing ourselves! Maybe that's why Jesus said "feed My sheep", I'm not totally sure.

Perhaps my favorite illustration of this is that when traveling on an airplane, during the safety briefing, they tell you that if the oxygen levels drop in the plane, masks will drop, and you should put your mask on before helping someone else. I want to say to the flight attendant giving the briefing - "Oh don't worry about that! Everyone is definitely going to be concerned about themselves first!"

Hopefully you are convinced of the fact that, well, we love ourselves. We've looked at one teaching on the idea of *self* from Scripture and several experience-based examples, but let's look at one more passage:

Let nothing *be done* through selfish ambition or conceit, but in lowliness of mind let each esteem others better than himself. Let each of you look out not only for his own interests, but also for the interests of others. Philippians 2:3-4

Look out not *only* for your own interests – God *assumes* here that we take care of ourselves. We are not commanded here to love ourselves. God knows we already do that. He assumes it. It's who we are. Congratulations – your self-care is perpetually on auto-pilot. Great job, you.

In fact, nowhere in Scripture are you told to love yourself. Think about that. Of all the things that God says to do and not to do in the Bible – all the important instructions that He knew we needed - "love thyself" is not one of them.

Self-worth is Found in Christ

The irony is that even though we love ourselves (perhaps a little too much), and God loves us because of who He is, the Bible says that apart from Christ - we really aren't all *that* lovable.

Some of you just had a visceral reaction to that last sentence, because this is counter cultural to how the world has tried to train us to think. Everything in our culture tells us that we are awesome. Everything tells us that we are worthy. Everything tells us that we are lovable just the way we are. There are even some *Christian* authors and bloggers who tell us that we are inherently *worthy* of God's love and care. But I'm not buying it.

That's not the teaching we find in Scripture. We are not inherently worthy of God's love. In fact, because of our sin, which has separated us from God, we lose our true purpose and worth. One of the best places this principle is illustrated is in the plight of the children of Israel in the book of Jeremiah. The history of the Jewish people, all throughout the Old Testament, follows the same cycle. It goes like this:

**Yay! we are following God → Oops! we are turning to sin →
Oh boy, we are experiencing God's judgment →
Ok, ok, we have decided to repent →
Yay! we are following God → Oops!**

The nations of Israel and Judah had a perpetual choice. Each generation had a choice in what they would do with the Lord. They had an opportunity to follow God or to turn away from Him. Let's look at a few examples, chronologically, of the choices they made during the time of Jeremiah:

> *As the thief is ashamed when he is found out,*
> *So is the house of Israel ashamed;*
> *They and their kings and their princes, and their priests and their prophets,*
> *Saying to a tree, 'You are my father,'*
> *And to a stone, 'You gave birth to me.'*
> *For they have turned their back to Me, and not their face.*
> *But in the time of their trouble*
> *They will say, 'Arise and save us.'*
> *But where are your gods that you have made for yourselves?*
> *Let them arise,*
> *If they can save you in the time of your trouble;*
> *For according to the number of your cities*
> *Are your gods, O Judah.*
> Jeremiah 2:26-28

Here we find that they have made idols of wood and stone their gods. They have as many gods as they have towns! Their idolatry was great. They had seemingly completely turned away from the Lord and had gone their own way. Verse twenty-seven describes their decision in a nutshell: they turned their backs to God and not their faces. What a description! What an accusation! And the sad thing is that they had a choice in the whole thing. God did not force these decisions on them. They made a conscious, purposeful choice to rebel.

We all have that choice in our own lives. We must all make the decision to accept or reject Christ. But for those of us who have trusted Christ, we have a decision every day to face God or turn our back on Him. Every morning we must make a decision to actively continue to follow Jesus Christ. And it's not easy to do this! Like Israel, everything around us wants to pull us away from following after Christ, to seek other things to worship and adore.

Here is another example of their idolatry - and the Lord's faithfulness in spite of it:

Go and proclaim these words toward the north, and say:
'Return, backsliding Israel,' says the Lord;
'I will not cause My anger to fall on you.
For I am merciful,' says the Lord;
'I will not remain angry forever.
Only acknowledge your iniquity,
That you have transgressed against the Lord your God,
And have scattered your charms
To alien deities under every green tree,
And you have not obeyed My voice,' says the Lord.
Jeremiah 3:12-13

Here we see God's command to Jeremiah to proclaim the need and opportunity for repentance to the Jewish people. God *wants* them to repent. He does not want them to be punished. All they must do is 'acknowledge' their 'iniquity'.

It is the same with us when we falter, when we fall. God is not looking to punish us. He is not waiting for His chance to strike us down with lightning. He loves us! He is merciful! He *wants* us to return to Him. He wants us to find our true purpose in Him. In fact, we find in chapter seven that God has again and again sent His Word to the Jews through His prophets, calling His people back to Him:

Thus says the Lord of hosts, the God of Israel: "Add your burnt offer-
ings to your sacrifices and eat meat. For I did not speak to your fa-
thers, or command them in the day that I brought them out of the
land of Egypt, concerning burnt offerings or sacrifices. But this is
what I commanded them, saying, 'Obey My voice, and I will be your
God, and you shall be My people. And walk in all the ways that I have

commanded you, that it may be well with you.' Yet they did not obey or incline their ear, but followed the counsels and the dictates of their evil hearts, and went backward and not forward. Since the day that your fathers came out of the land of Egypt until this day, I have even sent to you all My servants the prophets, daily rising up early and sending them. Yet they did not obey Me or incline their ear, but stiffened their neck. They did worse than their fathers. "Therefore you shall speak all these words to them, but they will not obey you. You shall also call to them, but they will not answer you.
Jeremiah 7:21-27

We see here God's faithfulness – every day He sent His prophets to speak the truth, to warn the people. God's desire for all people is repentance – including you and me.

And in perhaps the most poignant description of the Jewish people at this time, Jeremiah gives this thought in a conversation with God:

*You are near in their mouth
But far from their mind.*
Jeremiah 12:2

What a description of many Christians today! God is near in their mouth. They talk about Him, they go to church, they even give some money. But God is far from their heart, far from their thoughts as they go through their day.

So what is the point here? How does this all relate to a balanced view of self? Stay with me, and let's land this plane with a powerful example.

Over and over again, God gave Israel a choice. A choice to repent and turn back to Him. They would not do it. So, God uses a visual example to illustrate the severity of their decision and what it means for them. It is one of my favorite sections in all the Bible....

The Linen Sash

Thus the Lord said to me: "Go and get yourself a linen sash, and put it around your waist, but do not put it in water." So I got a sash according to the word of the Lord, and put it around my waist. And the word of the Lord came to me the second time, saying, "Take the sash that you acquired, which is around your waist, and arise, go to the Euphrates, and hide it there in a hole in the rock." So I went and hid it by the Euphrates, as the Lord commanded me. Now it came to pass after many days that the Lord said to me, "Arise, go to the Euphrates, and take from there the sash which I commanded you to hide there." Then I went to the Euphrates and dug, and I took the sash from the place where I had hidden it; and there was the sash, ruined. It was profitable for nothing. Then the word of the Lord came to me, saying, "Thus says the Lord: 'In this manner I will ruin the pride of Judah and the great pride of Jerusalem. This evil people, who refuse to hear My words, who follow the dictates of their hearts, and walk after other gods to serve them and worship them, shall be just like this sash which is profitable for nothing. For as the sash clings to the waist of a man, so I have caused the whole house of Israel and the whole house of Judah to cling to Me,' says the Lord, 'that they may become My people, for renown, for praise, and for glory; but they would not hear.'
Jeremiah 13:1-11

God tells Jeremiah to purchase a sash – a belt made of linen. And then He tells Jeremiah to go to the "Euphrates". We are not exactly sure because of the Hebrew wording – but we believe this is refer-ring to the Euphrates River (the word for "to Euphrates" and the word for "to [the village of] Parah" are the same in Hebrew). But, again, pretty certain that the Euphrates River is in mind given the context. By the way, this would have been a 700-mile (1,100km) journey of almost 8 months for Jeremiah to accomplish this task!

So, Jeremiah goes and hides the linen sash in the rocks near the river as commanded. And "many days" later – probably months -

God tells him to go and retrieve it. When he does, he finds of course that it is "completely useless". It has been ruined by time, by the weather, by the water, and by the sun. It is falling apart. It can no longer serve its intended purpose as an article of clothing.

Israel is the sash. The moral of the illustration is that the entire purpose of the nation of Israel was only found when they chose to "cling" to God. This purpose was three-fold:

1 - for renown (fame) of the Lord
2 - for praise of the Lord
3- for the glory of the Lord.

In short, they were to be an example to the world of their awesome God! But they "would not hear". They forgot their purpose. They turned their back on God. The linen sash is a representation of the fact that without God, Israel is nothing – completely useless.

So, how does this apply to us? The principle here is directly applicable. We have to know and live out our purpose – God's plan for us - to find our true worth. Without Him, we are useless. The idea of the illustration of the sash is that people who reject God are "good for nothing".

So, where does our worth come from? Not from ourselves! Our worth comes from knowing Christ and following Him:

Not that we are sufficient of ourselves to think of anything as *being* from ourselves, but our sufficiency *is* from God, who also made us sufficient as ministers of the new covenant,
2 Corinthians 3:5-6

You and I are not good enough to do anything without God. You and I have no purpose apart from Christ. In fact, I could do nothing apart from Christ:

for in Him we live and move and have our being,
Acts 17:28

Christ is the source of life and being! Apart from Him, we would have nothing! But, again, in contrast to this idea, the world tells us that we should love ourselves (we've covered that), and that we should promote and pursue healthy "self-esteem" – a high view of self. Let's examine that further.

Self Esteem vs. Self-Denial

"Esteem" means your opinion about something or someone, what you think about that person or that thing. Self-esteem is an individual's subjective evaluation of their own worth. Psychologists Smith and Mackie defined it by saying "The self-concept is what we think about the self; self-esteem, is the positive or negative evaluations of the self, as in how we feel about it."[2]

"Self-esteem" has been a big topic for the last several decades. It is still a huge topic in the spheres of education, psychology, parenting, and many other sectors. We are told that we need to have extremely high self-esteem or we simply cannot function, cannot be successful in this world and in our interactions with others.

Interestingly, the Bible says nothing about self-esteem as a value to hold. In fact, the Bible tells us to focus on just the opposite – not worrying about our *own* self-esteem, but to focus on *esteeming* others.

Let nothing *be done* through selfish ambition or conceit, but in lowliness of mind let each esteem others better than himself. Let each of you look out not only for his own interests, but also for the interests of others.
Philippians 2:3-4

---

[2] https://en.wikipedia.org/wiki/Self-concept

Lowliness of mind means humbleness. To be humble means to have a low estimation of your own importance in the grand scheme of things. So, God says, you don't need to spend time thinking highly of yourself. In fact, you need to make sure you are humble – you need to remember that you are not the most important thing on the planet. And then what are we to do in lieu of that revelation? *Esteem* – consider, think of – others as better than ourselves! God doesn't say anything about esteeming yourself – in fact, He says just the opposite. He *does* say that we should esteem others better than our own selves! The word *better* in those verses above means "of surpassing value"! That's how I should look at others around me. Self-esteem? Don't really have time for it, thanks. What God is really calling us to do is to deny ourselves.

> Then He said to *them* all, "If anyone desires to come after Me, let him deny himself, and take up his cross daily, and follow Me. For whoever desires to save his life will lose it, but whoever loses his life for My sake will save it.
> Luke 9:23-24

To deny yourself means to say no to yourself, to refuse to give yourself what yourself really wants. Does that sound like God telling us to love ourselves, and make sure we care for ourselves, and esteem ourselves as special and important?

Jesus said that I need to deny myself and take up my cross if I will follow Him! This is the very opposite of loving yourself, caring for yourself, worrying about yourself.

Don't look out only for your own interests – because we know you are doing that already, remember? But look out for, care for, and seek the good of others.

> Let no one seek his own, but each one the other's well-being.
> 1 Corinthians 10:24

This verse teaches the exact opposite of what the world teaches! To *seek* means to make an effort, or to try to accomplish something. God says you don't need to make any effort, you don't need to focus at all on yourself, on doing good for yourself – you and I will do enough of that anyway! Instead, focus on the good of others around you!

Promoting self-love is unbiblical, has no Scriptural foundation, and is unnecessary. It is also distracting to the real work of loving others. In short – it is a lie from Satan that you need to spend time and effort on loving yourself! Satan knows that you will care for yourself just fine, but if he can make you focus on yourself, lay down your cross, and forget about others, you will not and cannot be focused on serving Christ and others! And by the way, the ultimate way to love others is to share the gospel with them. What else could be more important to their well-being? But we cannot do that if we are focused on ourselves. A focus on self-esteem distracts from evangelism and discipleship.

The real way to love myself is to love God and love others. The real way to do the best for myself is to be involved in what God has saved me to do – good works for others. Caring for others is the ultimate way to care for yourself.

> I have shown you in every way, by laboring like this, that you must support the weak. And remember the words of the Lord Jesus, that He said, 'It is more blessed to give than to receive.'"
> Acts 20:35

If you want to be blessed, don't spend your day focused on yourself. Spend your day focused on others. As we do this, we are more like Christ than in any other way. He gave His life for others – for you and for me and everyone. And we should do the same.

Care for yourself, yes. God assumes that. But focus on others. God commands that. And in doing so, be your true self that God made you to be. That's the balanced view of self.

Small Group Discussion Guide

After reading the chapter discuss the following questions below.

1) Read Ephesians 5:29
What does this verse tell us? Do we love ourselves?

2) Read Acts 17:28
Where does our strength and ability come from?

3) Read Luke 9:23-24
What does it mean to deny yourself?
What does it mean to take up your cross?

4) Read 1 Corinthians 10:24
Who should we focus on?

5) Discuss and answer the following questions:
Have I been too focused on myself lately?
How can I focus on others this week?
Who can I love and serve this week?

CHAPTER 2

A Balanced View of Sin

The more we understand what the Bible says about sin, the better we are equipped to have victory over it in our own lives. But before we start fighting battles and slaying sin dragons, we need to back up and understand how our belief about sin – and about God – impacts our ability to do so. We need to think about sin as being something real – not some abstract concept or a theory of the universe – but a real enemy of sorts that we have to deal with.

Our first order of business on this part of our journey of finding our midpoint is to answer the question - what *is* sin exactly? If we don't know what it is, we won't recognize it in our lives and the lives of others. And if we don't recognize it, we can't overcome it very effectively in our daily lives.

Whoever commits sin also commits lawlessness, and sin is lawlessness.
1 John 3:4

Sin is breaking God's laws. Or, stated another way, without God's rules, there would be no sin. (This is how the majority of people live their lives, by the way).

for where there is no law *there is* no transgression.
Romans 4:15

Sin exists because God exists. Sin exists because God exists, and He has made some rules. Ponder that for a moment. What we know as sin is simply disobeying a set of rules that God has arbitrarily established, based on His character. He didn't ask anyone's opinion (certainly not mine or yours!) nor did He need too. He is the Creator and He....well, created the entire system. He makes the rules – whether you, or I, or anyone else likes it or not (and many people don't).

I think about it like a game we might play together. Every game has its own set of rules. *Uno* has different rules than chess, for example. My sons recently started teaching me how to play chess. I love it – but it is much more complex than *Uno*, to say the least. The moves are intricate, related, and consequential. And what you do as a player – every single move – matters. When you are playing the game of chess, you play by the rules. You are confined to that system, in other words. Whoever created chess built certain rules or "laws" into it. It is possible while playing the game to either play by the rules or violate the rules. I can think the rules are unfair (why is the *King* one of the weakest pieces?) but it doesn't matter. If I am playing chess, by definition I either adhere to or violate the rules based on my decisions. Where the game analogy breaks down is that if I am tired of playing chess, I can leave the board and go do something else, or I can play another game, or I can create my own game. I can alter my "game reality". Not so in life. Human beings have no ability to alter reality – what actually is. We may try. We may be deceived into thinking we can. But in truth, whatever moves I make, they are made inside of the reality of life.

In short, God makes the rules! God defines reality by His very nature and by His creation and His laws. Why is one thing considered a sin and something else not? I don't always know! And neither do you. But God has built the world this way, has built this into our very consciences, and has deemed that breaking His law is very serious (Romans 6:23). We can complain about the rules, try to circumvent them, try to ignore them, or call them obsolete – but they still remain.

Yet this is simply not the view of most people in the post-modern world in which we live. To harken back to the previous chapter, the post-modern man views *self* as an evolving, changeable product, not as a defined entity with real constraints. As author David Wells notes, "In this new world, the self is not something that *is*; it is something that is *constructed*." [3] And I would add, in this view of the world, sin may or may not exist, because God may or may not exist, self may or may not exist or be moldable, and reality is defined by each individual's understanding and experience as supreme. The post-modern view of self is a denial of reality, rooted in a denial of the Creator God, that leads to a dangerous (non)view of sin. It's no wonder that sin has its way in our world today – most people do not even perceive that there is a threat! Without understanding the reality of God, the reality of sin is incomprehensible.

My wife and I once took a self-defense course. It was very informative and as enjoyable as that sort of course could be. But one thing that stuck with me was something the instructor said at the beginning. After the usual introductions and pleasantries, he looked at each of us with a somber face and said, "when you leave this class you will see the world differently." I thought that was a bit of a bold statement for a half-a-day voluntary course – but he proved to be prophetic. During the course, our instructor taught us about the different levels of situational awareness. Developed by defense expert and marksman Jeff Cooper, the "Situational Awareness Color Code"

---

[3] David Wells, *God in the Wasteland: The Reality of Truth in a World of Fading Dreams* (Wm. B. Eerdmans Publishing, 1994), 99.

contains four different levels: white, yellow, red, and black. In white, you are relaxed and not aware of what is happening in your environment. In yellow, you are still relaxed but you are aware of who and what is in your personal environment: you have a "lay of the land". In condition Orange, you have identified something that may (possibly) pose a threat and are actively observing that person or thing. If that thing or person actually does something threatening to you, you move to condition red, which is a "threat verified" level of readiness for self-defense.

COLOR CODE OF AWARENESS

WHITE (unaware)	You are relaxed, completely unaware, and unprepared.
YELLOW (situationally aware)	You are relaxed, have an alert mindset, and are aware of your surroundings.
ORANGE (potential threat)	You are in a heightened state because something just doesn't look or feel right.
RED (ready to fight)	There is a verified threat and it's time to take action and execute necessary fight.

What I came to realize during the course, is that most of the time I was walking around in "condition white" - totally unaware of what was going on around me and my family. As I have since realized through subsequent training and experience, this is an unwise place to camp out in. If you haven't noticed, the world is a dangerous place. It is simply wise to be aware of that and aware of your surroundings. Yet most people walk around, like I did, totally unaware of what is happening around them.

While most people have a "general awareness" of the concept of sin (whether they accept it or not mentally, their conscience bears witness), they have no awareness of the *specific* sins that are lurking just around the corner of *their* life. Either they have subscribed to post-modern thinking and attempt to create their own truth, or they believe in God but are oblivious to the real power of sin. They are practically unaware that they have a real Enemy, who wants to use real tactics to bring real destruction to their life.

A better place to be is to be in condition yellow – situationally aware. Not panicked. Not worried. Not living in constant fear of sin (this leads to legalism, but I digress). Instead – actively aware of the threat. Aware of sin's menacing potential. This level of spiritual awareness lends itself to identifying temptation and potential sins and meeting them head-on with prayer and Scripture. We must maintain the constant spiritual discernment that sin is very real, very prevalent, and very possible for each of us to participate in.

Now that we understand a little more about sin and its relation to reality, we can focus on the major problem. The BIG problem is – *none* of us play by the rules.

for all have sinned and fall short of the glory of God.
Romans 3:23

And it's been that way...well...from the beginning. The very first man and woman were basically operating at awareness level "white" (look at that cute little snake! Oh, he talks!). By the time the situation had advanced to color red, it was far too late.

Then the Lord God took the man and put him in the garden of Eden to tend and keep it. And the Lord God commanded the man, saying, "Of every tree of the garden you may freely eat; but of the tree of the knowledge of good and evil you shall not eat, for in the day that you eat of it you shall surely die."
Genesis 2:17

So, when the woman saw that the tree *was* good for food, that it *was* pleasant to the eyes, and a tree desirable to make *one* wise, she took of its fruit and ate. She also gave to her husband with her, and he ate. Then the eyes of both of them were opened, and they knew that they *were* naked; and they sewed fig leaves together and made themselves coverings. Genesis 3:6

Very clearly, we see the command of God – the law - in Genesis chapter two. And then we see lawlessness – breaking that command - in Genesis chapter three. Sin had entered reality.

Again, most people are generally aware of sin as it affects their personal, daily lives. They *are* aware that something is broken and needs repairing. That's the reason for so many religions in the world. Religion is man's answer to try and repair the sin problem, without really understanding the nature of that problem. But most people in our world do not fully understand the true gravity or pervasiveness of sin.

Sin is not "making a mistake". I don't like when people say that, and I think it's an imbalanced, unbiblical view of sin. You make a mistake when you color outside the lines on a coloring book page. But it not just a mistake when you intentionally transgress the law of Almighty God. It is a willful, purposeful defiance of God through your thoughts or actions. A sin is you communicating to God "I don't care what you say, I want to do this, this will feel good, this will make me happy, this will benefit me, so I'm doing it anyway". That's what goes on in our hearts and minds when we sin. Does that sound like an accident to you? Does that sound like "just a little mistake?" Mistakes are unintentional. Sin is on purpose.

Once you understand the seriousness of sin as direct disobedience to God, you have an easier time understanding why sin carries consequences. Once you realize and accept that God makes the rules – not you – you have an easier time with understanding that your actions have consequences. Your moves on the board have results. Sometimes those results are not even anticipated. Several times while learning to play chess, my boys would sweep in for a move and I would exclaim "I didn't even see that!". "Sorry, Dad." We often don't expect the consequences that our sin will bring until they are upon us.

The terrible thing about all this is that sin is not a one-hit wonder when it comes to paying up. Oh no. Like a greatest hits album, sin is the enemy that keeps on giving. Let's look at a few of the consequences that sin brings into our lives.

Consequence: Sin Brings Confusion

One of the consequences of our sin is confusion.

> This I say, therefore, and testify in the Lord, that you should no longer walk as the rest of the Gentiles walk, in the futility of their mind, having their understanding darkened, being alienated from the life of God, because of the ignorance that is in them, because of the blindness of their heart;
> Ephesians 4:17-18

Many of us have been in a funhouse mirror maze at a fair or carnival. If you've never had the experience, it is all at once hilarious and confusing. Hilarious, because you cannot find your way out no matter how hard you try. Confusing, because you cannot find your way out no matter how hard you try. After a while in a funhouse, for me, it loses its appeal. The frustration starts to outweigh the hilariousness and I start to feel that I just want to get out and move on to the next ride. The confusion becomes annoying and disorienting and frustrating. Imagine living your entire life stuck in a mirrored funhouse, where every move you make seems right in the moment, but turns out to be wrong – very wrong. Where what seems like a fun part of the game at first, turns out to be a very bad decision. Before long, you don't even know where you started, how you got to where you are, or where the exit is. That is a life filled with sin.

Sin has that same way of confusing you. You rationalize that what you are doing is okay, when in reality it's not. You may even think that you are doing the right thing! Look at the key words in the verses from Ephesians above: darkened.... ignorance.... blindness. *That* is what sin does to a person who is controlled by it.

Often a person who is enslaved to sin is so confused they cannot see the way out. Someone who is addicted to drugs cannot find out how to stop – they are blinded to the Truth and the only One Who can help them. Someone who is living an immoral life is often in the worst relationships and dealing with difficult personal situations, and they are blind to what is causing their problems – their own lust and sinful desires. Those may be two extreme examples, I understand. But if we are living in any kind of perpetual sin, we are most likely blinded to what it is really doing to us. We are confused, disoriented, and wondering why we cannot seem to find blessing in our life. Sounds like a great time, doesn't it? If Satan is anything, he is the world's best marketer, making sinful actions seem like they hold the answer, when in reality they simply carry us further from the Truth.

Consequence: Sin Brings Shame

Then the Lord God called to Adam and said to him, "Where *are* you?" So, he said, "I heard Your voice in the garden, and I was afraid because I was naked; and I hid myself."
Genesis 3:10

One of the immediate effects of sin for the child of God is shame. Think about the last time you sinned – whatever situation that was. You may be the only one that knows about it. Yet what was the ultimate result? If you are a Christian, the answer is: shame. In these moments, along with Ezra we can surely say....

"O my God, I am too ashamed and humiliated to lift up my face to You, my God; for our iniquities have risen higher than *our* heads, and our guilt has grown up to the heavens
Ezra 9:6

Sin promises us excitement and wonder. In the end it brings shame and dishonor.

I'll never forget the moment that my child became a *Smurf*. My oldest, Reece, was around two years old, and he was being "unusually quiet". Every parent knows the horror of this unwelcome silence. It can only mean one thing – mischief.

I walked into Reece's bedroom, did not see him, and noticed the light in the adjacent bathroom was on. As I walked in to switch it off, I had a sense that something was amiss. You know how you can "feel" another person in a room? (Oh come on). Somehow, I knew he was behind the door, though I couldn't see him, and I don't recollect that he made any sound. As I opened the door to the bathroom and looked around behind it– there, up on the counter, hidden just moments before by the door, was my blue son. Blue from head to toe. He had found the sponge "bath paint" that we let him use under normal bath time circumstances– with adult supervision – to draw on the bathtub walls. But on this day, he had decided that he himself would be a much better canvas for his artistic endeavors. But that's not the funny part of the story.

Immediately, when I laid eyes on him, a shocked yet amused expression came across my face. And immediately upon seeing that expression, Reece paused, stared at me, and then in one beat, instantly began to cry uncontrollably, inconsolably. It was hilarious.

It was funny because he was not really in trouble – he was just being a kid and had not disobeyed any specific command. I knew that, but he did not. And so, I cannot help but laugh even now at his dismay. But where did his episode of crying really come from? It came from shame. He knew – even at two years old – that mom and dad – his authority figures – would not approve of his current situation. No matter how much fun he had (I still have no idea how long he was at it or how fast it all progressed), in the end the lingering result was shame and dishonor. I think you see the correlation.

Consequence: Sin Brings Bondage

> Jesus answered them, "Most assuredly, I say to you, whoever
> commits sin is a slave of sin.
> John 8:34

Sin, if we willfully submit to it, enslaves us. It becomes our master
– our king. This is a doctrine that should sober every person. Sin has
an almost living power – a personification of sorts – to act on us and
our will. Sin is not a static theory that we can sit on the shelf and take
up again when we choose. Sin is a dynamic force – a force of evil that
holds sway over those who do not know Christ and His power over
it.

Martin Lloyd Jones in describing sin says, "This thing that has entered into our very nature and constitution as human beings, is
something that is so polluting our whole being....". [4]

The idea of sin being an active force is not something out of a Star
Wars movie. It is straight from the life and writings of the Apostle
Paul himself. In Romans he writes:

> But I see another law in my members, warring against the law
> of my mind, and bringing me into captivity to the law of sin
> which is in my members.
> Romans 7:23

When Paul uses the term "law" he does not mean the Mosaic law.
He means a principle, or a force that is actively engaged. He "sees"
or has experienced this power in himself, and it wars against his own
spiritual desires and has the potential to make him a prisoner to its
principles. Indeed, Paul says in other places (Romans 7:17) that this
sin – this law, this power, this force – dwells in him.

---

[4] Meyer, Jason. Lloyd-Jones on the Christian Life. Wheaton, IL: Crossway, 2018.

We cannot trivialize or minimize the active power that sin has to bring bondage, even to our lives as believers. If we submit to it as master, it is present, ready, and able to take control – to enslave. And a slave is not free to choose his own path. Even if he wants too, he must obey the master. The master holds power over him.

Consequence: Sin Brings Death

> For the wages of sin *is* death...
> Romans 6:23

Sin brings physical death and spiritual death. When God told Adam that he would die if he ate the tree – He meant that Adam would die physically, yes – but also *spiritually.*

An old quote says, "sin fascinates and then it assassinates". Sin assassinates the entire person – the spirt, the soul, and the body.

In summary, sin is a serious reality for all of us. It is not something to be diminished or laughed off. Sin brings confusion, shame, bondage, and death – quite the laundry list! Sin is not something to be trivialized, laughed at, or swept under the rug of our days. Sin is the reason that Jesus came to die.

Freedom from Sin

Now at this point in our discussion of balance, you may be a little bit dismayed as you consider the greatness of the power of sin to control, undermine, and destroy your life. But that is exactly the perspective you must have to achieve the true biblical, balanced understanding of the doctrine of sin. To appreciate the real hope of your life station you must understand the despair that could have been your lot instead. Understand the seriousness of sin and you will understand the greatness of our Savior!

> For the wages of sin *is* death, but the gift of God *is* eternal life
> in Christ Jesus our Lord.

Romans 6:23

There is only one Way to be free from the power of sin, and His name is Jesus! When we trust in Christ, God removes the power of sin over us through the blood of Christ, and we are free to serve Him and worship Him with our lives:

Likewise you also, reckon yourselves to be dead indeed to sin, but alive to God in Christ Jesus our Lord. Therefore do not let sin reign in your mortal body, that you should obey it in its lusts. And do not present your members *as* instruments of un-righteousness to sin, but present yourselves to God as being alive from the dead, and your members *as* instruments of righteousness to God. For sin shall not have dominion over you, for you are not under law but under grace.
Romans 6:11-14

The word "reckon" means to consider something, to keep a record of something. The idea is keeping an account of something, like a financial record. You know the account balance. You know the status.

A lot of people don't know how much money they have in their bank account. They just charge things to a credit card and are then surprised at the end of the month when they cannot cover the balance. But there is really no excuse. If your bank is like mine, you are constantly reminded of your balances. I get texts, emails, app notifications, paper statements in the mail – all designed to inform me of my account status. Every time you go to the ATM the bank gives you a receipt. It tells you your account balance. That receipt is your *reckoning*. It is the *status* of the account – the reality of the money there.

God says that you should reckon yourself - consider yourself – know the true status of yourself – as being dead to sin. It means that sin has no real power over you anymore. You have the ability to choose the right path, the righteous path. Because you are alive to God in Christ Jesus! You have life to choose God's path. This is the difference between a believer and unbeliever. The believer has the power over sin!

Finding Balance

This is the balanced, biblical view of sin in the life of a believer. Is sin a powerful force that has the ability to destroy our lives and families? Is it something that we should be aware of, even wary of, in hopes to avoid it? Yes, and yes. These things are still true for those of us who trust in Christ.

At the same time, do we have the power that is greater than sin living in us, that makes us able to conquer sin and defeat it – as if it was deadened in its power and we were dead to it – not even able to interact with it? Yes!

Do not let sin reign. The word "reign" means to be a king, or to have complete control. Most people out in the word have sin as the king of their life. They follow whatever feels good, whatever looks good, whatever will make them happy. They obey sin like they obey a king. Instead, we as believers can present ourselves to God ready to serve Him in righteousness, using our minds and our bodies for good things, not evil things.

> Don't you realize that you become the slave of whatever you choose to obey? You can be a slave to sin, which leads to death, or you can choose to obey God, which leads to righteous living.
> Romans 6:16 NLT

The big idea is this: as a believer, you have a choice. You have a choice to live for God. But it is not automatic. You must choose every day to follow Christ, every day to make Him – not sin – King of your life.

Sin has only as much power as you allow it to have. If you allow it, sin can still have great power over your life. So, don't minimize sin. Don't just say "I made a mistake". You are fooling yourself. You are opening yourself up to more and more sin. Perhaps the biggest mistake of Christians is minimizing the raw power that sin has the potential to unleash. A weakened view of sin is out of balance biblically. It is not the view that Jesus has of our Enemy, or that any of the human authors of the New Testament had. We must take sin seriously in our lives and in the lives of those we love.

But the balance is this: sin can have no real power over you, through the blood of Christ, if you don't allow it to. We are not to walk around with a defeatist attitude, thinking that we cannot help ourselves, or taking a "the Devil made me do it" posture. We are to respectfully, reverently refuse to give sin the power that it desires to have.

So have a balanced view of sin in your life, Christian. Don't fret about the potential power of sin over you, but at the same time don't be so prideful that you think you cannot fall into it. It is a paradox – sin is powerful, but sin is powerless. Find the healthy midpoint, the biblically colored awareness of sin in your life. Balance.

Small Group Discussion Guide

After reading the chapter discuss the following questions below.

1) Read 1 John 3:4.

What is sin? Write out a definition of sin in your own words:

2) Discuss the four consequences of sin from the chapter.

Have you experienced these consequences personally?

3) Read Romans 6:11-14.

What does it mean to be dead to sin?

What does it mean to be alive to God in Christ?

Does sin have power over a Christian? Why or why not?

CHAPTER 3

The Balance of Hearing and Doing

Take heed to yourself and to the doctrine. Continue in them, for in doing this you will save both yourself and those who hear you.
1 Timothy 4:16

On Being a Hearer

In his inspired letter, Paul is instructing Timothy to pay close attention to his life and to the teachings of the Bible. The lesson for us is clear. We must continue in the doctrine – the teaching of God's Word - if we will grow as a believer. You cannot grow as a Christian and ignore your Bible.

Be diligent to present yourself approved to God, a worker who does not need to be ashamed, rightly dividing the word of truth.
2 Timothy 2:15

In other words, work hard in understanding the Word of God, so that you do not need to be ashamed when it is time to apply it. Know how to handle the Bible for your own life, and as you disciple others, helping them apply it to theirs. "Rightly dividing" means literally 'to cut straight'. Don't take things out of context. Know exactly what passage can apply to what situations – or at the very least know where to look to find the answer! It is crucial to know your Bible if you will have a victorious Christian life. The two cannot be separated!

Jesus said this:

If you love Me, keep My commandments.
John 14:15

But how can you keep what you do not know? Our measure of hearing is directly responsible for the level of our ability to *do*. Without knowing God's Word, we cannot keep it.

Hearing Leads to Rest

Hebrews chapter four is very instructive in our discussion of hearing and doing. In this chapter, the writer is warning his readers not to fall into the same trap of unbelief and lack of faith as the Israelites did.

For indeed the gospel was preached to us as well as to them; but the word which they heard did not profit them, not being mixed with faith in those who heard it.
Hebrews 4:2

The Jews heard the truth of God as we do, but they did not believe it – they did not "mix it with faith" so as to make it profitable to themselves. Because of this, they did not find rest, but they wondered in the wilderness of their sins for many years.

There remains therefore a rest for the people of God. For he who has entered His rest has himself also ceased from his works as God did from His.
Hebrews 4:9-10

The Bible says here that we should have rest, we should have peace, as we have faith in Christ, as we live our lives trusting the Lord. The *rest* that is being discussed is the rest that God gives to believers who trust in Christ. The Bible compares it directly to the rest that God took after the creation of the universe: the word translated "rest" in Hebrews 4:9 is *sabbath* – the same rest that God took when He rested after creation. It is not a rest of complete inactivity, for God is still active today. It is a rest following completion. God had completed His creation and it was good. As believers we rest – we sabbath - in the completed work of Jesus Christ on the cross.

Let us therefore be diligent to enter that rest, lest anyone fall according to the same example of disobedience. For the word of God *is* living and powerful, and sharper than any two-edged sword, piercing even to the division of soul and spirit, and of joints and marrow, and is a discerner of the thoughts and intents of the heart.
Hebrews 4:11-12

The writer warns us that we must be diligent – careful – that we have entered this Sabbath rest that only comes through Jesus Christ. He warns that there is a danger of falling into the same unbelief and lack of faith as the Jewish people. And how can we enter into this rest? Answer: by listening to God's Word.

According to these verses, this warning about missing God's rest is based on the nature of the divine revelation. The Bible's claims cannot be dismissed. God has given us what we need to live eternally, to live fully, and we *must* listen to Him! We cannot argue with God! We cannot choose our own path; we cannot live our own way and choose our own consequences! The implication is that full rest is not possible unless the Word of God is followed. Sabbath will not be realized until the Word has permeated every area of your life. We must follow Christ to truly have rest in our life. And to follow the Word and trust the Word, you must first know the Word. Christian, you must learn the Word. You cannot live for God if you don't know what God expects of you. Yes, you can learn to live for God by following the example of other believers. But you must also learn directly from God what He expects from *you*. If for no other reason, let us commit to learning, memorizing, knowing, and living God's Word so that we may find His rest.

The Power of Hearing

For the word of God is living and powerful....

Living. The Bible is not some old dusty book that only pastors and grandparents are interested in. It is a living revelation that has constant application to our daily lives. I hear some ministry leaders talk about wanting to make the Bible relevant for today's culture. I have news for them. The Bible is always relevant, because it is living, it is alive! It meets our needs today just as much as it did a hundred years ago or a thousand years ago.

Powerful. That word means "active" and "effective". When you study the Bible, it does not leave you where it found you. God's Word demands a personal decision about what it says. You either decide to follow and live God's way, or you decide to reject it, but you must decide.

.....and sharper than any two-edged sword, piercing even to the division of soul and spirit, and of joints and marrow, and is a discerner of the thoughts and intents of the heart

The Word is so powerful that the writer compares it to a two-edged sword, or a dagger. A two-edged sword is able to penetrate, is able to cut faster, than a single edged sword because it is working in both directions simultaneously. The Bible is more effective than a two-edged sword to penetrate our lives, our minds, and our hearts. The Bible penetrates our very souls and our spirits. It permeates all of our life.

The human being is made of 3 divisions that all interrelate – body, soul, and spirit.

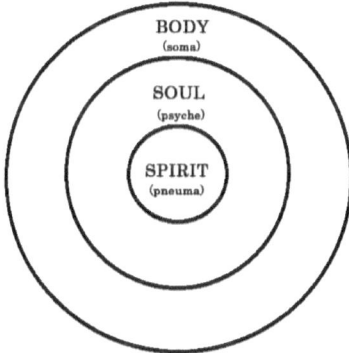

Your body (the Bible uses the Greek *soma*) is, of course, your *physical* being. Your five senses are activated and controlled by your *soma*.

Your soul (Greek: *psyche*) is your inner being, your personality – your thoughts, your mind, your emotions.

Your spirit (Greek *pneuma*) is that part of you that is able to commune with God.

The Word of God engages *every* part of our being, and it even helps divide the soul and spirit which so often get mixed together in our understanding. For example, sometimes what passes for worship is not really worship of God from your spirit - but some sort of emotional reaction from your soul. How do we recognize this? How do we discern things like this? The Word of God helps us, teaches us, guides us. Or, sometimes we may feel that we are making the right Spirit-guided decision, but really it is our own thoughts and desires guiding us and not the Holy Spirit. How can we discern the difference? The Word of God separates the two so we can see clearly. Those are just two examples, but I think you get the picture.

When the Bible says "joints and marrow" it means that the Word does not miss any part of us. It is thorough! It is to our core! As deep as it can go! In fact, the Word discerns our very thoughts and intentions. In quick time, the Word will show you what you really are. Now, the question is: what will you *do* with that information? With that, let's talk about being a doer.

On Being a Doer

All Christians fit into one of three categories when it comes to hearing and doing:

1 – they don't hear at all
They are not faithful in church, never read their Bible, etc.

2 – they hear and do
They are faithful to absorb truth often and work to apply it

3 – they hear and forget
They listened with good intentions, but never make application

Those in category one pose a different set of problems that we will save for perhaps a different time. Our concern here is finding the correct balance of hearing and doing. And the book of James is instructive when it comes to doing, telling us of two options that exist: living the Word or forgetting the Word.

But be doers of the word, and not hearers only, deceiving yourselves. For if anyone is a hearer of the word and not a doer, he is like a man observing his natural face in a mirror; for he observes himself, goes away, and immediately forgets what kind of man he was. But he who looks into the perfect law of

liberty and continues in it, and is not a forgetful hearer but a doer of the work, this one will be blessed in what he does.
James 1:22-25

The Word of God is a mirror for our life. It gives us information. But it is not enough just to see the information. We must take what we see and use it. We must apply it. We must live it. And if we live it, we will be blessed. Simple to understand. Harder to do.

When you wake up in the morning and you look in the mirror - it's not enough just to look at yourself and walk away. At least not for me. You must do something with the *information* you have just been given by the mirror. You need to brush your hair for goodness sakes. You need to change your clothes. You definitely need to brush your teeth. Some mornings, the signal may be so strong that you just need to go back to bed! Whatever the mirror is telling you, you need to take action or there is no point in having a mirror at all.

In the same way, it is not enough to merely hear God's Word – either during the weekly Sunday sermon or when you read it yourself during the week – and not do anything about it.

Too many Christians substitute hearing for doing. But it is not the hearing that brings the blessings but the doing. I can read a verse that teaches me that I need to love my wife; but if I don't take action to *show* her love, I will not have any of the blessings of a good marriage that are offered.

The Bible here calls itself "the perfect law of liberty". The Word of God brings liberty – freedom – to our lives - when we apply it and live it. When we stay within it's boundaries, we find freedom to be who God intended us to be – fulfilling His purpose.

One of my favorite verses about the impact of God's Word applied is this one:

And I will walk at liberty,
For I seek Your precepts.
Psalm 119:45

The word *liberty* here literally means "a wide place". When I hear and then seek to live His Word, God will make my life like a broad plain, full of good choices and options, a life free and overflowing with blessed paths every day!

Now, back to James. You really cannot get any more plain or straight forward than James 1:22. In fact, there is a biblical bias towards applied knowledge throughout Scripture. God doesn't just want you to fill your head with knowledge – He wants you to fill your head with knowledge and then apply that to your life! God wants us to have a balance in our life of gaining knowledge and applying knowledge. It is not enough just to know a lot of things but do nothing with that knowledge. It's not enough just to sit and listen to a sermon but never have any intention of actually applying it. We call these people "sermon sippers" – they take a little drink of this sermon, a little drink of that sermon, and just continue to fill themselves without ever pouring out – without ever serving, without ever growing, without ever applying it. Some of you reading this book have been sipping sermons, reading books, and learning the Bible for years, but not doing anything with what you know. It's time to change that! I'm not mad at you – I want you to have the joy that comes from applied knowledge – from being a doer.

James 1:25 says that we should *look into* the Word – it means "to stoop down, to take a close look". This is an interested and sustained look with an intent to apply. When you read something in the Bible or hear something preached that makes a lightbulb go on – pause, take time, stoop down – and find a way to make a change in your life in accordance with that truth. In this, you will become a doer.

The Balance

We have explored the importance of hearing and the necessity of doing. Now we need to land the plane and talk about balance between these two.

First, I hope it is clear that the Bible is biased towards action, towards applying knowledge. But it is important to remember that action by itself is not the goal. Some Christians seem to accomplish a lot of ministry, and yet they spend very little time with the Lord. The power is removed from their ministry in these situations. Jesus said, "without Me you can do nothing". We must abide in Him – we must be with Him – if we will be successful in serving Him. And what is involved in abiding in Him?

> If you abide in Me, and My words abide in you, you will ask what you desire, and it shall be done for you.
> John 15:7

Jesus connects His Word abiding in us with spiritual power and effectiveness. We see in this verse both hearing and doing, working together and informing each other. This is important.

Let me illustrate this importance with a story from the book of Luke:

> Now it happened as they went that He entered a certain village; and a certain woman named Martha welcomed Him into her house. And she had a sister called Mary, who also sat at Jesus' feet and heard His word. But Martha was distracted with much serving, and she approached Him and said, "Lord, do You not care that my sister has left me to serve alone? Therefore tell her to help me." And Jesus answered and said to her, "Martha, Martha, you are worried and troubled about many things. But one thing is needed, and Mary has chosen that good part, which will not be taken away from her."
> Luke 10:38-42

Here we have Martha the doer and Mary the hearer. In this passage, is Jesus saying that one is right and one is wrong in how they are living their lives? Did Jesus say that Martha was wrong for serving? No. Serving is not wrong. In fact, Jesus teaches us to serve. Jesus said that Martha was "distracted with *much* serving" or, in other words, "anxious with *a lot* of ministry".

The idea is that Martha had too much to do. Why was it too much? Because she did not have time for the Lord. He was teaching her (and us) that she was out of balance. Her priorities were not in order. She was not focused at all on Jesus and His teachings. She was just focused on *doing*.

It is possible to be in ministry and serving the Lord and be so busy that you do not have time for the Lord. Think of that! You are out of balance. Have you ever been out of balance in this way? I have! It's not a place I want to stay when I find myself there.

Instead, we should strive to find the right balance. And that is what I want you to see – the balance of hearing and doing. It is not either/or. It is not that we should choose one over the other. It is that we must choose both! We should imitate Martha in our service and Mary in our worship – simultaneously, in balance. [5] Do not be a hearer only. But also, do not be a doer only. Both of these extremes are out of balance! Instead, be both a hearer and a doer – and be blessed!

---

[5] Wiersbe, Warren. *Bible Exposition Commentary*. Wheaton, IL: Victor Books, 1996.

Small Group Discussion Guide

After reading the chapter discuss the following questions below.

1) Read 1 Timothy 4:16.
What are the two things we should pay close attention to?

2) Read 2 Timothy 2:15.
What does "rightly dividing the word of truth" mean?
Why is this important?

3) What are some ways that we can be *hearers* of God's Word?

4) Read James 1:22-25
What is the balance taught in this verse?
Is this balance a struggle for you? How?

5) Discuss the story of Mary and Martha (Luke 10:38-42)
What was Jesus teaching here?
How does it apply to me?

The Balance of Faith and Works

How much of the Christian life is faith and how much is works? Is doing something a requirement to be saved, to remain saved, or not? Just believing is enough, right? In this chapter we will address all of these questions as we consider the appropriate, biblical balance of faith and works.

A Mature Faith

If we are going to talk about faith, we need to define what that is.

"Faith is hearing God's Word, believing God's Word, acting on God's Word, and leaving the rest to Him."
– Dr. Bill Monroe

That definition from my Pastor, Bill Monroe summarizes a biblical understanding of faith. If you will notice, the definition includes hearing *and* doing – taking some sort of action on what you've encountered (for more on this refer to chapter three). Many times, we don't think about action, or works, being part of the defining attributes of true faith – but it is! That's why James says that "faith without works is dead". True biblical faith includes all three components: hearing, believing, and acting.

Each of us who are believers in Christ would say that we want our faith to grow. We want to become mature in our faith. But the challenge is – the path that we would choose for ourselves to accomplish this is not necessarily the one that God chooses for us. And that has a tendency to throw some people off course, discourage them, or make them give up altogether. As we will see, the path to mature faith is often filled with trials, temptations, and hard work.

Trials from Without

> My brethren count it all joy when you fall into various trials, knowing that the testing of your faith produces patience. But let patience have *its* perfect work, that you may be perfect and complete, lacking nothing.
> James 1:2-4

In these opening verses, James addresses the issue of trials that come from *outside*. Later, he addresses temptations that come from *inside* our own hearts. But here he is talking about trials that we "fall into" – meaning they are often unexpected things that we encounter; literally, the unforeseen events of life that we do not plan for or wish to happen. The picture is a little bit like falling when you step into a hole or stumble over something in the way – no one *plans* to do that!

The Bible here says, *"various* trials", meaning this can include many different things. It may include physical trials, financial difficulties, relationship issues, gossip, broken hearts – the list goes on! It can include personal danger or tragedies. I can't list them all here, but you get the idea.

For most of us, trials *naturally* produce a negative attitude – often an attitude of complaining. Someone does something negative to me and my first thought is "why did You let that happen, Lord?". And I complain and I feel sorry for my situation. For example, almost any time I get sick I think "why did this have to happen *now*; I have things to do!"

But God says our perspective on trials should be something very different. He says we should have joy when we face a new trial. Joy! Not only joy, but God says to count it "all joy". It means not a little joy mixed with some complaining thrown in on the side for good measure. *All* we should have is joy in a trial!

Does that sound kind of ridiculous to anyone? I mean, *really,* God? Really? My child gets sick and I am supposed to be joyful in that situation? I lose my job and I am supposed to have joy in that time in my life? Someone hurts me deeply by something said or done and I am supposed to react with overflowing joy? Really?

Really.

Ok ok, so how can we actually achieve this high-water mark as believers? The answer is given as the verse continues.

...knowing that the testing of your faith produces patience

To know something means to understand it. And as Christians, we must understand that God has a bigger plan for us than just this moment right now - bigger than just the trial that we find ourselves in. In fact, we must remember that God is doing something *good* for us in and through that trial.

Trials in our life are really a test that God brings into our life to grow our faith – to purify and mature our faith. Trials have a purpose – to produce patience in our life. And having patience makes us "perfect and complete" – exactly what God wants us to be! A mature faith is a patient faith – a faith that trusts in God no matter what. What God wants in my life is for me to believe Him no matter the situation. And He brings trials into my life to teach me to have patience and trust Him.

I heard of a grandmother who, anytime one of her grandchildren was complaining, would call them over and say, "Yes child, there, there. You just sit right here and tell me all about how God didn't keep His promises to you". Cleared the situation right up usually, from my understanding. It's very much about perspective.

You must learn to see the trials in your life through the right perspective – through a biblical lens. These difficulties in your life are not accidents that God is not aware of! God has allowed them specifically to refine you and shape you and sanctify you! *This* knowledge is the key to having joy in a trial.

Now, I am fully aware that this is easier said than done. Which I believe is why in the next verses James tells us that if we don't understand how to do this, we can ask God for wisdom to do it:

> If any of you lacks wisdom, let him ask of God, who gives to all liberally and without reproach, and it will be given to him.
> James 1:5

It's human to struggle with trying to see the long view in a difficult situation. It's natural to have a hard time finding the joy when something terrible is happening. It's spiritual to come to God and ask Him for the wisdom to see and act according to His Word.

Now, not to throw more obstacles in the path to mature faith, but we must consider that not only do we encounter trials from the *outside*, we encounter trials of our own making – temptation from *inside* our own hearts.

Temptation from Within

As Christians we can severely hinder our spiritual growth by allowing external trials in our life to overwhelm us, discourage us, distract us, and derail us. But, we can also fail to grow in Christ by falling into sin when we are tempted.

Blessed *is* the man who endures temptation; for when he has been approved, he will receive the crown of life which the Lord has promised to those who love Him. Let no one say when he is tempted, "I am tempted by God"; for God cannot be tempted by evil, nor does He Himself tempt anyone. But each one is tempted when he is drawn away by his own desires and enticed. Then, when desire has conceived, it gives birth to sin; and sin, when it is full-grown, brings forth death.

James 1:12-15

Let's talk about temptation.

Temptation is the opportunity to participate in a bad thing, or to participate in a good thing in the wrong way. Satan is described in the Bible as the "tempter" in Matthew 4:3. Certainly he plays a role in tempting us to sin. But Satan is not the only one to blame. Our own hearts have sinful desires that can tempt us. When I am "drawn away" by those desires, I am in trouble, and very close to sin. The picture is of luring a fish out of hiding with a bait.

I love to fish. I have a lot of fishing gear that I've collected over the years. I had mentioned that I loved to fish to my wife when we were dating, but I perhaps did not share the full scope of the situation. When she finally laid eyes on my fishing gear stored in my Dad's garage she was dumbfounded. She could not believe how many different rods, reels, lures, tackle boxes, thing-a-ma-jigs, and watcha-ma-call-its that she saw. While probably not totally defensible (we all have our struggles), in all seriousness – most of it was necessary to be a successful fisherman. I know that if I want to lure a fish, I need to be ready with multiple different types of lures, different types of rods to cast those lures differently, and differing presentations for each lure as it is cast to account for the weather, water temperature, spawning patterns, and environment of the particular location. There's a lot that goes into successful fishing! What a fisherman is trying to do is to "draw away" a fish from his cover, his safe space, and entice him with just the right lure presented in just the right way in the exact right season.

Our heart does the same thing.

And yet, being tempted by something is not sinful. Jesus Himself was tempted by Satan, as we read in Matthew. In fact, Jesus was tempted in every way that we are while He was on the earth:

> For we do not have a High Priest who cannot sympathize with our weaknesses, but was in all *points* tempted as *we are, yet* without sin.
> Hebrews 4:15

Again, being tempted by something is not a sin. Temptation leads to sin when the desire "has conceived", or you allow the desire to turn into action. It's not a problem for the fish to notice a passing lure. It's a problem when he takes action and gets hooked.

We see in James 1:12 that it is possible to endure temptation – to remain steady, to stand firm in our beliefs and to not fall (for more on this see chapter 2). Interestingly, the word for *endure* in verse twelve is very close to the word for *patience* back in verse two. The glaring truth is that if your faith is not mature, if you have not been tested and learned patience, it will be harder for you to endure temptation. If you have not learned to trust the Lord, to lean on Him and not your own understanding and heart, then you will be tempted and take action on every lure that passes by!

These verses also do not leave us any room for blame shifting – James tells us very clearly that God is so Holy that He cannot even be tempted by sin, and that He is not the One Who tempts us. So, we can't blame it on Him!

> Do not be deceived, my beloved brethren.
> James 1:16

Deceived means "to miscalculate or reason falsely". You think you know what's going on when are in the middle of temptation and subsequent sin, but you don't. The danger is that no temptation appears at first glance to be a temptation. The fish doesn't know it's a lure. The fish thinks it is dinner. Satan's tactic is to deceive you and me into thinking that there is a better option out there than the one God has given us. It was his first trick in the garden – Satan tempted Eve to think that maybe there was something God was not telling her – maybe there was a better way! Satan tempts us to listen to the desire in our own heart – that it must be good, it seems so right! But James has laid out the birth process of sin, and we should not be deceived by ignoring it.

> Every good gift and every perfect gift is from above, and comes down from the Father of lights, with whom there is no variation or shadow of turning. Of His own will He brought us forth by the word of truth, that we might be a kind of firstfruits of His creatures.
> James 1:16-18

God brings good things into our lives! There is no shadow of turning with God – He never turns His back on you or me! And of His own will, He has saved us through the Word of Truth – the Gospel of Jesus Christ! Remembering the goodness of God and believing Him is a bulwark to helping us resist giving in to temptation in our lives. And learning to trust Him in trials and temptations is the beginning of the path to mature faith.

Qualities of Mature Faith

A mature faith is active in doing

We've already briefly examined James 1:22-25 in the chapter on hearing and doing, but it also applies to the balance of faith and works, so let's look at it again from that angle.

But be doers of the word, and not hearers only, deceiving yourselves. For if anyone is a hearer of the word and not a do-er, he is like a man observing his natural face in a mirror; for he observes himself, goes away, and immediately forgets what kind of man he was. But he who looks into the perfect law of liberty and continues *in it,* and is not a forgetful hearer but a doer of the work, this one will be blessed in what he does.
James 1:22-25

What kind of faith do you have? Is it a mature faith? Is it the kind of faith described in James chapter one? An active faith that is not only hearing but doing as well? The important thing is not to try to manufacture bigger faith, but to simply place your faith in the right Person. Maturity is not about the amount of your faith – it's about the *placement* of your faith.

if you have faith as a mustard seed, you will say to this moun-tain, 'Move from here to there,' and it will move; and nothing will be impossible for you.
Matthew 17:20

The mustard seed was the smallest seed known in the world at that time. This phrase was used at that time to describe things very small or very little. All you need is a little faith – in the right place!

A mature faith is full of love

My brethren, do not hold the faith of our Lord Jesus Christ, *the Lord* of glory, with partiality. For if there should come into your assembly a man with gold rings, in fine apparel, and there should also come in a poor man in filthy clothes, and you pay attention to the one wearing the fine clothes and say to him, "You sit here in a good place," and say to the poor man, "You stand there," or, "Sit here at my footstool," have you not

shown partiality among yourselves, and become judges with evil thoughts?
James 2:1-4

Imagine for a moment that you are sitting in your church's Sunday morning worship service. The service has not quite started, and people are still milling about, talking and fellowshipping. Then you notice one of the most well know, successful, richest, and philanthropic couples in the whole city, and they are visiting for the first time and apparently looking for a place to sit. You have open seats right beside you. What would you do? Some of us would choose to be very helpful and assist this wonderful (and very rich) couple. Some of us would be scared to death to "make the first move", but would be elated if they chose to sit near us. We would instantly feel more important just by their presence. Now think of the same scenario, except instead of the wealthy, famous couple, you notice that guy who, on any given day, is usually seen pushing his grocery cart down the street with a dog chained to it. By the looks of him he has been drinking, and his clothes are clearly dirty – and he is looking for a seat. You have one available next to you. What do you do?

James is challenging the church to not become a VIP club - only concerned about connecting and serving the people that are deemed important by societal and cultural standards. If we do this, we create a false narrative – judging that there is a difference between one person and the next. In verse four, James calls this difference evil. It is evil to think that one person is better than another person.

In the church I pastor in Marikina City, Philippines we do have people that come into our church that are living on the street. We have had people that are maybe not completely coherent mentally walk in on a Sunday. That is a reality of our mega-city. We have people that visit who don't smell very good. They like to talk to me for some reason. But the overriding question is - how do we *really* view people when we encounter them? Are we more concerned with outward appearance than looking at the heart of a person – seeing their spiritual needs?

Our God does not view people with partiality:

Yet He is not partial to princes,
Nor does He regard the rich more than the poor;
For they *are* all the work of His hands.
Job 34:19

Jesus did not respect people based on their outward appearance or their ability. Even His enemies were aware of this:

Teacher, we know that you are true and teach the way of God truthfully, and you do not care about anyone's opinion, for you are not swayed by appearances.
Matthew 22:16b

I'm glad that Jesus didn't look at me for just what I *was,* but instead for what I could and can be. Jesus sees the greatest potential in the greatest of sinners. And He calls us to do the same.

Now this chapter is not just about greeting different people when they walk into the worship service. That is just the one example that James uses to illustrate the larger truth. The main point is that people of mature faith in Christ are to love others.

If you really fulfill *the* royal law according to the Scripture, *"You shall love your neighbor as yourself,"* you do well; but if you show partiality, you commit sin, and are convicted by the law as transgressors.
James 2:8-9

Why is partiality a sin? Jesus illustrated in the parable of the Good Samaritan (Luke 10:25-37) that *everyone* is our neighbor. As Warren Wiersbe wrote, "It is not about geography, but about opportunity".[6] When we have the opportunity to do good for someone, we should do it. Because we are to love everyone! We are to accept everyone! Christian love is treating everyone the way God has treated me, *especially* those on the outside of the fellowship.

The danger for any church or any Christian is turning inward and focusing on people who are already with us, when in reality we should be focused on reaching everyone, everywhere! Genuine faith reveals itself in how we love and serve all others around us.

A mature faith is full of action

What *does it* profit, my brethren, if someone says he has faith but does not have works? Can faith save him? If a brother or sister is naked and destitute of daily food, and one of you says to them, "Depart in peace, be warmed and filled," but you do not give them the things which are needed for the body, what *does it* profit? Thus also faith by itself, if it does not have works, is dead.
James 2:14-17

Now we come to the heart of this chapter – the balance of faith and works. And we can see in the place that we have now arrived logically, that true faith absolutely must include works – tangible actions. A mature faith has as it's siren song a love song. And love is an action.

Does it help a hungry person if I say to them "don't be hungry anymore!" with a big smile and full of joy and enthusiasm, but give them no food? No! In fact, we would say that's crazy – it doesn't make sense. Because we inherently understand the correlation of action and impact – that works are required to actually make a difference. So, James compares this situation to faith without any kind of life change – without any kind of good works as evidence. What

---

[6] Wiersbe, Warren. *Bible Exposition Commentary*. Wheaton, IL: Victor Books, 1996.

benefit is it if you have faith without any actions to go with your faith? Can that *kind* of faith save you? The answer is.... no.

Saying you want to help someone but not doing anything about it means that your thoughts, words, and even intentions are empty. Taking no action means that you were not genuine. Just saying you have faith but having no evidence of that faith, does you no good. That *kind* of faith is not genuine, not alive – it is dead. Action is the evidence of genuine, mature faith. A genuine faith is full of action – full of good works!

Imagine that you had a goldfish, and the fish died. A sad thing. And you were sad. And you told your friend about it. And you were sad together. And you had a little funeral for the fish. And while you are both standing there in awkward silence, you friend taps you on the shoulder and says "look, your fish is alive again"! And you open your eyes and......there is no movement, no life, nothing. Still floating upside down. The *claim* of your friend would be refuted by the *evidence* before you. Your friend can continue trying to comfort you (or perhaps make fun of you) by telling you your fish is alive, but the evidence proves he is wrong. In the same way, we can claim to have faith in Christ, but the real test is: what does the evidence show?

> Show me your faith without your works, and I will show you my faith by my works.
> James 2:18b

James gives a summary of this whole chapter. He literally means "out of my works you will see my genuine faith".

If you are serving the Lord – active in what you believe in your heart – that is evidence that your faith is genuine. But if you are never doing anything for the Lord, if you don't have any desire to come to worship Him, you don't spend time with Him in His Word, you are not abiding in Him, you don't love others, you have no pattern of good works for the Lord – you need to examine yourself and your faith to see if it is genuine. The truth is this: we only believe as much of the Bible as we practice. You can disagree with me on that, but that is exactly what James is saying here. You can say you believe God's Word, but if you make no attempt to live by it – your confession – God says - is not genuine.

James even brings up the faith of Abraham to make his point, and this is where the idea of faith and works can get a little confusing if we aren't careful:

Was not Abraham our father justified by works when he offered Isaac his son on the altar?
James 2:21

So, James says Abraham was justified – effectively given eternal life, biblically speaking– *by works.*

In the book of Romans, Paul also references Abraham and he writes this:

For if Abraham was justified by works, he has *something* to boast about, but not before God. For what does the Scripture say? *"Abraham believed God, and it was* accounted to him for righteousness.
Romans 4:2-3

Paul is directly referencing Genesis 15:6 and saying that Abraham was *not* justified by works – but *by faith.* Hmmm. So, James says Abraham was justified *by works* and Paul says he was justified *by faith.* So.... was Abraham justified by faith or by works? Who is right? Is one of them wrong?

They are both right. Stay with me. James would agree with what Paul wrote here, and Paul would agree with what James wrote as well. They are really emphasizing two different parts of the same truth. Paul's main point is that we are not saved by working for it – we are saved by faith in Jesus Christ. James is saying that our faith in Jesus Christ will not be alone – it will have works as evidence. He goes further to explain in the next few verses:

Do you see that faith was working together with his works, and by works faith was made perfect? And the Scripture was fulfilled which says, *"Abraham believed God, and it was accounted to him for righteousness."* And he was called the friend of God. [24] You see then that a man is justified by works, and not by faith only.

James 2:22-24

James says that Genesis 15:6 – which talks about belief – was fulfilled when Abraham's works evidenced that his faith was genuine. His works showed that his faith was complete. In fact, the word "only" in James 2:24 is best translated as "alone". Thus, John Calvin wrote: "It is therefore faith alone which justifies, and yet the faith which justifies is not alone". In other words, we are not saved by faith *plus* works, but by a faith *that* works. That is Paul's point and that is James' point, and it is the balanced, coherent truth of the Scripture. A genuine mature faith is never alone – it will be full of good works – full of action. And one of those actions that the Bible talks about *a lot* is the act of speaking. Let's camp there for a moment and consider the power and impact of our words.

Words as Actions

When we speak it has power. Words have consequences. We often think of actions being something physical, tangible, or easily seen, but the words we say are also a form of activity that reflect the faith in our hearts.

Words have the power to bring direction

My brethren, let not many of you become teachers, knowing that we shall receive a stricter judgment. For we all stumble in many things. If anyone does not stumble in word, he *is* a perfect man, able also to bridle the whole body. Indeed, we put bits in horses' mouths that they may obey us, and we turn

their whole body. Look also at ships: although they are so large and are driven by fierce winds, they are turned by a very small rudder wherever the pilot desires. Even so the tongue is a little member and boasts great things.
James 3:1-5

The words that we say have great power. Our words have the ability to encourage, to guide, to give wisdom. We can provide comfort to the hurting, direction to the lost, and guidance to the timid. The power of speech is one of the great blessings of God in our lives. With positive, encouraging speech I can correct and guide my children. I can encourage and lift up my wife. I can preach the gospel. Speech is also very important for a leader – with speech leaders cast vision, give directions, delegate tasks to be accomplished, and encourage followers.

We must be careful with this power. The tongue is a very small part of your body, and yet it perhaps wields the most power. Just like a gigantic ship that is turned by a very small rudder. One small adjustment on that rudder can have a big impact over time on the course of the ship. In the same way, our words – even a few words - can make a big impact. Speech that is spoken at the right moment, for the right reasons, is a beautiful thing.

A word fitly spoken *is like* apples of gold
In settings of silver.
Proverbs 25:11

I can remember in Junior High sitting on the side of the soccer field after P.E. class, and our coach Brad Bochette encouraging us in a Bible study with the truth that we could do whatever God made us to do, because He gives us the power and ability to do it. I've never forgotten that lesson! I was so inspired. Just the same, I've never forgotten my 7th grade English teacher Mrs. Moore telling me that I was a good writer. It made a huge impact on me!

Words have great power to influence the direction of someone's life. Just imagine – a conversation that you have in passing or a lesson that you teach one random Sunday morning may stick with a person for decades and come to shape their life! Incredible!

However, words can also have a negative impact. In World War 2, the Allies had a phrase warning of the power of words: "Loose Lips Sink Ships". It meant that one person talking about their knowledge of a fleet's schedule or deployment plans could result in the enemy hearing about it, causing a disaster and potentially effecting the outcome of the war. Just a few words determining the outcome of a global war! Imagine that!

Words can also hurt people. You can damage the very soul of a child by what we call "verbal abuse" – always telling the child they are not smart, they are ugly, etc. Many children grow up in a highly negative verbal environment and as a result have a large hill to climb when it comes to their image of themselves.

Death and life *are* in the power of the tongue
Proverbs 18:21b

Maybe you have heard the phrase "sticks and stones can break your bones, but words can never hurt you". That is one of the cutest, memorable, stupidest phrases to ever be uttered in the English language. Words can *absolutely* hurt! Words have the power to bring destruction.

Words have the power to bring destruction

See how great a forest a little fire kindles! And the tongue *is* a fire, a world of iniquity. The tongue is so set among our members that it defiles the whole body, and sets on fire the course of nature; and it is set on fire by hell. For every kind of beast and bird, of reptile and creature of the sea, is tamed and has been tamed by mankind. But no man can tame the tongue. *It is*

an   unruly   evil,   full   of   deadly   poison.
James 3:5b-8

When I was a kid in the 90's, I think every third commercial on TV was a *Smokey the Bear* commercial. Come on, say it with me: "only you can prevent forest fires". That's a lot of pressure to put on an eight year old, don't you think, Smokey? I'm the only one? But in all seriousness, the intention behind the campaign was genuine and smart. Smokey knew, and he taught all of us, that a small spark from an untended fire could cause a thousand-acre inferno. A cigarette flicked carelessly out of the window could burn an entire country-side. You can burn a whole forest with just a small initial flame – just an ember. And James compares the tongue to that small flame – it can bring destruction to an entire life, an entire family, even a whole church!

Here is how James describes the tongue (our speech):

- **a fire** – has the ability to bring great destruction.
- **a world of iniquity** – it is an entire universe of wickedness
- **defiles the whole body** – your mouth can get you into trouble that then involves your whole body. Saying the wrong seductive things can lead to sexual immorality. Saying the wrong angry words can lead to physical fights.
- **sets on fire the course of nature** – this means the whole course or path of your life. It can affect your entire world and the world around you.
- **untamable** – to tame means to bring under control. Don't think that you can control your speech on your own– God says you cannot!
- **unruly evil** – it is unstable, restless, not content to be still and quiet
- **full of deadly poison** – deadly poison does not always kill instantly. Sometimes with poison it is a slow, painful death. And the same is true with destructive words.

Encouraged yet? This is quite the description of the thing that lives in your mouth and gets in the way of you brushing your teeth sometimes. If all this weren't enough, Jesus tells us in Matthew where this kind of destructive speech actually comes from:

> But those things which proceed out of the mouth come from
> the heart, and they defile a man.
> Matthew 15:18

If we have negative, destructive speech on our tongues it is really coming from our hearts. So, think about the last time that you lost control of your temper – you were very angry at someone, shouting, etc., or the last time you said something hurtful to a family member. Where did that come from? It came, Jesus says, from your heart.

> For out of the abundance of the heart the mouth speaks
> Matthew 12:34

What does the word *abundance* mean? It means an overflow or plenty. What is in your heart is what comes out of your mouth. It spills over, it overflows. Whatever is in there is what will spill out. My pastor always says, "what is down in the well comes up in the bucket".

James says that the tongue is "set on fire by hell". What does he mean? The source of the sinful speech that comes out of our mouth is Satan himself, the first one to rebel against God and the first one to tempt Eve to sin against God. This fire does not come from God – it comes from Satan and our sin nature that his wiles introduced into the world.

What is coming out of your mouth on a regular basis? Is it anger? It is complaints? Is it negativity? As believers we should not allow this fire to rage out of control. That is the point James makes in the next section, because our words have the power to bring goodness and life.

Words have the power to bring delight

With it we bless our God and Father, and with it we curse men, who have been made in the similitude of God. Out of the same mouth proceed blessing and cursing. My brethren, these things ought not to be so. Does a spring send forth fresh *water* and bitter from the same opening? Can a fig tree, my brethren, bear olives, or a grapevine bear figs? Thus no spring yields both salt water and fresh.
James 3:9-12

James is stating the uncomfortable truth that believers – often in the span of a few minutes – can praise and worship the Lord and in turn wish evil on their fellow men. And it should be impossible for this to occur. And yet it will occur if we are left to ourselves. In fact, as believers we must recognize that we cannot control our tongues; we must rely on the Holy Spirit and the Word to help us in this matter. If Jesus is the King of my heart, my speech will reflect that. If I am yielded to the Holy Spirit, and I have His fruit in my life, my speech will reflect that.

But the fruit of the Spirit is love, joy, peace, longsuffering, kindness, goodness, faithfulness, gentleness, self-control.
Galatians 5:22-23

Think about the fruit of the Spirit in relation to our speech: loving speech, joyful speech, peaceful speech, patient speech, kind speech, good speech, faithful speech, gentle speech, controlled speech. Can you see the difference in that kind of speech and a speech that is a wild, raging fire that consumes a person and the people around them? Our speech has the great potential to bring delight to our lives and to those around us.

Here are some good words to say often that we teach to our children but take for granted ourselves:

- **Thank you** – speech that shows appreciation
- **I'm sorry** – speech that shows humility
- **I love you** – speech that shows admiration
- **I'm praying for you** – speech that shows concern and care

The ultimate delight that words can bring is when we share the Word of the gospel. In John chapter one, Jesus is referred to as "the Word". He is the supreme communication from God, the best news one could ever hear. Paul calls the gospel "the power of God unto salvation" in Romans 1:16. The words of salvation! Are you sharing this good news with others? Are your words bringing delight and life to other people?

Remember, our faith is shown genuine by our works – and those works include our speech. It is not enough to simply know what you *should* be saying – you need to actually say it! We must bring loving, gospel filled speech to our tongues and thereby put our faith where our mouth is.

Warning: The Prideful Christian

To close this chapter on balancing faith and works out, a warning. When we being to mature, learning how to live a faith that works, and are aware of that we are doing so, we are primed to fall prey to that original sin that we thought was behind us: pride.

Where do wars and fights *come* from among you? Do *they* not *come* from your *desires for* pleasure that war in your members? You lust and do not have. You murder and covet and cannot obtain. You fight and war. Yet you do not have because you do not ask. You ask and do not receive, because you ask amiss, that you may spend *it* on your pleasures. Adulterers and adulteresses! Do you not know that friendship with the world is enmity with God? Whoever therefore wants to be a friend of the world makes himself an enemy of God. Or do you think that the Scripture says in vain, "The Spirit who dwells in us yearns jealously"? But He gives more grace. Therefore He says:

"God resists the proud,
But gives grace to the humble."
James 4:1-6

The word *pleasure* here is the Greek word *hedone* (hay-doh-nay), from which the term "hedonist" is derived. Hedonism makes man's pleasure the chief end of existence. In other words, in a hedonist's view, pleasure is the ultimate goal. The danger is that all of us can be classified as hedonists at some time or another. We all go through times (daily? hourly?) where our own satisfaction and happiness and pleasure are the most important things to us. This is really a part of a prideful mindset, a prideful heart. When I make my own pleasure my main goal, I am really focused on myself, thinking that I deserve such things or that I have earned this or that.

Lust comes from a desire for pleasure. Lust – *desiring something passionately and without restraint* – is a powerful word for a craving, a passionate desire. In modern terms, we most often think of a sexual lust, but the word means more than just that. It means anything that one might seek or desire with intensity – including sex, food, money, position, power, fame, etc. And the believer who lusts and chases after these things cannot really get them in the end – because they are not lasting, they are fleeting.

So, a prideful Christian serves himself, and this lust for pleasure is the cause of quarrels, fights, problems in the church, and conflict in the home. A prideful Christian does not ask God for help – they think they are self-sufficient. Or, when they *do* ask God for something, they are asking for their own benefit and not the benefit of others, the church, or God's glory.

What is pride? Pride is choosing your own comfort over service. It is saying "I am more important than anyone else". And pride is the currency of this present world. It is how the majority of people operate and live their lives. They may be nice about it! But they are working for number one – themselves! This is what God describes as "friendship with the world" – to be following the patterns and priorities of the world system. Satan is the ruler of this world for the time being (John 12:31), and his original sin was pride. He tempted Eve with pride. And he tempts believers today with pride.

This kind of attitude – a selfish, prideful mindset – makes one a friend of the world and an enemy of God. James says that God resists – is opposed to – this kind of *Christian*. Wow! James uses very strong language – calling them adulterers! It is spiritual adultery for the Christian who is a part of the church – the bride of Christ – to have an illegitimate relationship with the world, seeking after pleasure instead of serving God.

> Do not speak evil of one another, brethren. He who speaks evil of a brother and judges his brother, speaks evil of the law and judges the law. But if you judge the law, you are not a doer of the law but a judge. There is one Lawgiver, who is able to save and to destroy. Who are you to judge another?
> James 4:11-12

What does it mean to judge? It means to make decisions about other people's decisions. To judge someone else when you are not the King or the Lawgiver means either you do not trust the law that is given, or you do not trust the Judge. You are instead trusting yourself to make the determination. This is rooted in a prideful attitude! A prideful Christian trusts himself to make judgements about someone, instead of praying for that person and trusting God as the Lawgiver and Judge. This is a big one and so easy to fall into on a regular basis! How many times do I look at someone's situation and make a judgement about that person? "He should have done this instead" or "they should not have said that". I am becoming the judge of that person's life and actions. Literally, James says, "Who made you the judge?".

Our churches would be much healthier and happier if we would each devote our energy to obeying the Word instead of worrying about whether others are! When you see something negative in a person's life, don't talk *about* them to others (speaking evil), pray for them, confront them if necessary, and help them in love!

> Come now, you who say, "Today or tomorrow we will go to such and such a city, spend a year there, buy and sell, and make a profit"; whereas you do not know what *will happen* tomorrow. For what *is* your life? It is even a vapor that appears for a little time and then vanishes away.
> James 4:13-14

Another indication of a prideful attitude is self-confidence. How often are we self-confident in our travel plans, our schedule for the year, our business projections? We are many times very self-confident that we can "make it happen." What James reminds us of here is that man's plans are *always* tentative. A prideful Christian is confident in themselves and does not consider what the Lord would have them to do.

This is important for Christian leaders to understand particularly. A leader's main job is making decisions. And a leader must be confident in those decisions. But where should my confidence be placed as a leader? Not in myself! In the Lord!

One indication of self-confidence is a lack of prayer when making decisions. Do you give major time in prayer to major decisions? Another indicator is a lack of wise counsel from mentors and spiritual leaders. Do you seek counsel from people as you move through your life, or do you think "I know what is best"?

Promise: The Humble Servant

How are we to heed this warning and combat the very real possibility that we could fall into a prideful way of living? In contrast to this prideful, self-confident Christian, James presents the humble Christian.

> Therefore submit to God. Resist the devil and he will flee from you. Draw near to God and He will draw near to you. Cleanse *your* hands, *you* sinners; and purify *your* hearts, *you* double-minded. Lament and mourn and weep! Let your laughter be turned to mourning and *your* joy to gloom. Humble yourselves in the sight of the Lord, and He will lift you up.
> James 4:7-10

A desire for pleasure kills the will to serve. When a prideful person is only concerned about their own pleasures, they have no room to serve the Lord. They have no room to submit to the Lord. But a humble Christian submits his will, his desires, his pleasure to God. Submission is what it means to be a servant. You are not living out your own pleasure or desires, but living your life for the good of another, to the obedience of another.

A humble Christian does not pray and ask God for things to fulfill his own contrary desires. His prayers are filled with prayers for ministry, for others, for the lost, for the church! Even in prayers for himself he prays with the spirit of "Thy kingdom come, Thy will be done"! A humble Christian does not serve himself; he serves the Lord!

A humble Christian also does not judge others. They trust God to be the Lawgiver and Judge that He is, and they focus on their own walk with God and serving Him. They live and believe that:

"God resists the proud,
But gives grace to the humble

If I trust the Lord with my life, it means I trust that He is going to provide and care for me in His grace.

Humble yourselves in the sight of the Lord, and He will lift you up.

When I trust the Lord, I know that He will recognize and honor my humility. I know that the way up is down. Warren Wiersbe wrote that "grace is for the lowly not the lofty".[7]

Too many Christians derive their joy from the things of the world. Their laughter and fun come from material things, money, experiences, pleasure. And God calls us to purify our hearts from these things, to reject our prideful attitudes, and mourn and weep over our sinfulness. Too many of us are filled with the things of the world and could care less about what God wants for our lives. This should cause us great sadness, even mourning. And when we get to this place of mourning for our tendency to turn away from God and seek friendship with the world, then we have humbled ourselves and God will lift us up.

Do I think this does not apply to me? Then it applies ever greater! We need a revival; we need a fresh perspective of how important our relationship with God is! Our life is just a mist! It is here today and gone tomorrow!

> For what *is* your life? It is even a vapor that appears for a little time and then vanishes away. Instead you *ought* to say, "If the Lord wills, we shall live and do this or that." But now you boast in your arrogance. All such boasting is evil. Therefore, to him who knows to do good and does not do *it,* to him it is sin.
> James 4:14-17

On Suffering and Deliverance

As a final point of thoroughness, we must touch on suffering as a necessary partner of faith that works. Because if you have true faith that has accompanying works, you will also have trials and suffering to go along with that balanced faith. The Christian life is not about

---

[7] Wiersbe, Warren. *Bible Exposition Commentary.* Wheaton, IL: Victor Books, 1996.

always having the right circumstances, but about always having the right perspective.

Expect the Suffering

Come now, *you* rich, weep and howl for your miseries that are coming upon *you!* Your riches are corrupted, and your garments are moth-eaten. Your gold and silver are corroded, and their corrosion will be a witness against you and will eat your flesh like fire. You have heaped up treasure in the last days. Indeed the wages of the laborers who mowed your fields, which you kept back by fraud, cry out; and the cries of the reapers have reached the ears of the Lord of Sabaoth. You have lived on the earth in pleasure and luxury; you have fattened your hearts as in a day of slaughter. You have condemned, you have murdered the just; he does not resist you. James 5:1-6

James here is describing the trials that have come into the believer's lives as a result of persecution and oppression by the rich people in the society at the time.

First, it is important to know that God is not condemning wealth here, but rather the means of obtaining that wealth and the use of that wealth. It is not wrong to be wealthy, but it is a sin to become wealthy by cheating. These people had gotten their wealth by not paying their workers and servants. And apparently, some of these poor workers were Christians in the church.

Second, they were accumulating their wealth only for themselves. They "heaped up treasure' – it means to store it, to save it, to hoard it. They had millions in the bank, and yet they refused to pay their debts and their workers. They lived in luxury – wanton living – buying anything and everything they wanted with no regard for what the Lord would have them to do. Not only that, but they were using their wealth to influence the courts and even have innocent people, church members, sentenced and put to death.

James uses this one example to illustrate a larger point: trials in our lives are guaranteed. Some of the Christians in the church were not being paid for their honest labor. Some were being jailed and killed fraudulently. These were major trials happening in their lives, in the church!

There have been recent, well circulated reports that major U.S. candy companies have been using chocolate in their candies that originated directly from harvesting by child slaves in Africa. While shocking, is this true? Well, maybe, maybe not. No one really knows because there is so much deception in the entire supply chain, that even a visit on the ground by inspectors can be misleading in its findings. So, does that mean we do nothing? No, we are called as Christians to stand up for injustice, to stand up for the weak, to defend the fatherless. But at the same time, we do those things with regards to the reality that there will be no justice on a large scale until Christ returns. We must expect the suffering, for ourselves and for others. We can and do try to mitigate it, but we must remember that we live in a broken world.

In the world you will have tribulation;
John 16:33

We must through many tribulations enter the kingdom of God.
Acts 14:22b

Yet there is a balance (as always!). God brings the balance to our suffering through the Hope that He offers.

Anticipate the Deliverance

James writes that "the cries of the reapers have reached the ears of the Lord of Sabaoth.". Yahweh – the Lord of armies - has heard their cries! He will come to their rescue! He says that the rich oppressors had fattened their "hearts as in a day of slaughter". This was an ironic nod to the fact that the sheep who were to be killed on the altar were first eating all they wanted, living pleasurably. The fate of the oppressors would be the same.

> Therefore be patient, brethren, until the coming of the Lord. See *how* the farmer waits for the precious fruit of the earth, waiting patiently for it until it receives the early and latter rain. You also be patient. Establish your hearts, for the coming of the Lord is at hand. Do not grumble against one another, brethren, lest you be condemned. Behold, the Judge is standing at the door!
> James 5:7-10

God tells the persecuted, oppressed Christians what to do in light of their situation: be patient. Now, that is probably not what you want to hear when you have a big problem! I'm sure it is not what those with family members in jail wanted to hear. I'm sure it's not what you or I want to hear when we have a major financial problem, or health problem, or relationship problem. But James was opening their eyes to the reality of the Christian life: this world is not our home! Our hope is that this world is not all there is! Our hope is that in the end we will have the victory! Our hope is that Christ is coming back again to restore order and justice to this world and set up His Kingdom that will have no end!

To encourage us, we have four illustrations of patience and endurance in the face of trials:

Endurance: The Example of Farmers

> See *how* the farmer waits for the precious fruit of the earth, waiting patiently for it until it receives the early and latter rain. You also be patient. Establish your hearts, for the coming of the Lord is at hand.
> James 5:7-8

The farmer has to have a lot of patience! The farmer has to be at the mercy of the weather. If the sun is too hot, his crops may burn. If there is no rain, he may have no harvest. If there is too much rain, the crops will drown! I would be nervous all week if I was a farmer! Yet farmers are patient. They wait. They know that the rain is coming. They know the harvest is coming. And I know that God is producing a spiritual harvest in my life. And I am to wait patiently on Him. *Establish* in these verses means "to determine, to be fixed". Trust the Lord, that He is doing something good in your life, even in the drought, even in the trials. We know that all things work together for good for believers! (Romans 8:28)

Endurance: The Example of the Prophets

My brethren, take the prophets, who spoke in the name of the Lord, as an example of suffering and patience. Indeed we count them blessed who endure.
James 5:10-11a

Read through the Old Testament and see the suffering that God's servants the prophets went through! What we most often face pales in comparison, even in rough times! We should lean on this great cloud of witnesses as an example to inspire our own endurance.

Endurance: The Example of Job

You have heard of the perseverance of Job and seen the end *intended by* the Lord—that the Lord is very compassionate and merciful.
James 5:11

Job experienced great losses as Satan attacked him:

- His cattle were stolen and servants killed

- His sheep and servants were killed by fire from Heaven
- His sons and daughters were killed when a storm destroyed the house they were in
- He had painful boils from his feet to his head
- His wife told him to "curse God and die"

Pretty bad situation. Every reason in the world to give up. But Job endures. He remains faithful to God. In the end, Job survives, and God actually blesses him with double the possessions that he started with! If Job can make it through, so can you and I! None of us has ever had as bad a day as Job had!

Endurance: The Example of Christ

Lastly, Jesus is our ultimate example in endurance and perseverance, and we must look to Him for inspiration to continue pushing forward.

> Therefore we also, since we are surrounded by so great a cloud of witnesses, let us lay aside every weight, and the sin which so easily ensnares *us,* and let us run with endurance the race that is set before us, looking unto Jesus, the author and finisher of *our* faith, who for the joy that was set before Him endured the cross, despising the shame, and has sat down at the right hand of the throne of God. For consider Him who endured such hostility from sinners against Himself, lest you become weary and discouraged in your souls.
> Hebrews 12:1-3

Finding the biblical mixture of faith and works in our own lives is an ongoing process. Sometimes we have too little faith; sometimes we try too hard; sometimes we are prideful; sometimes we follow our flesh and not the Spirit. But when we prayerfully, daily work at striking the right balance – when we continue to grow and change, learn and do – then, at the end of the road, we find endurance.

At the end of the book of Revelation, it describes what the new heaven and new earth will be like:

And God will wipe away every tear from their eyes; there shall be no more death, nor sorrow, nor crying. There shall be no more pain, for the former things have passed away."
Revelation 21:4

Then our faith will be sight, and our works will be rewards. Until then, balance.

Small Group Discussion Guide

After reading the chapter discuss the following questions below.

1) Read James 1:2-4.
What does God say should be our response to trials?
What is the purpose of trials in a believer's life?

3) Read James 1:12-15.
Is it wrong to be tempted by something or someone?
Is it possible for a believer to have victory over temptation? How?

4) Read James 3:1-5.
How is our tongue like a rudder of a ship?
James says people who control their words are "perfect". What does he mean?

5) Read James 4:1-6
Where do fights and arguments come from?
What does it mean to have friendship with the world?

6) Read James 4:13-14
How would you describe this kind of person?
What does it mean that life is like a vapor?
Why is that important to know?

CHAPTER 5

The Balance of Vision and Contentment

The Bible talks a lot about vision and having a plan for the future. On the other hand, it also talks about being content with where we are. I've often thought about the seeming paradox that these clear teachings of Scripture present. How can I be content - satisfied with where the Lord has me - and yet still have vision, drive, plans, and desires to achieve more, move forward, and do great things that are currently undone? How can I have this kind of driven mindset and also maintain a spirit of contentment? They seem to be competing values. How do these things reconcile?

To answer that, first we need to define the terms *vision* and *contentment*, and then take a look at how they dance together.

What is *vision*?

Vision is the ability to see what could be rather than what is.

A leader with vision sees the changes needed around him (and many times in himself!) and looks to lead in those areas to affect change. A person with vision is driven by a picture of a preferred future.

One of my favorite illustrations of vision is Walt Disney's dream to build Disney World in Florida. Everyone thought he was crazy, including his family and close associates. The part of Florida that Disney wanted to place his theme park in was nothing but empty swamp land and orange groves. But he had a vision for it – a picture in his mind of what it would be. Sadly, Walt died before Disney World opened to the public. As the story goes, at the opening of the park, someone remarked to Walt's brother Roy with a well-intentioned comment that it was "sad that Walt did not live to see the park completed". Roy replied smartly along the lines of, "He did see it. That's why we are standing here today". That's vision.

Vision precedes ALL accomplishment. If you completed anything good without first thinking of it, planning for it, and acting on those plans, then whatever happened was not an accomplishment, it's a "happy accident", to quote the great Bob Ross.

One of the most fascinating things to me about vision is the process of something that is ethereal - just an idea - turning into a tangible reality. In fact, everything physically tangible in our world did not start out that way – everything started out as just an idea in someone's head. An artist, or an engineer, or an architect, or a computer nerd, or someone, somewhere had an idea. And as that idea ruminated in their minds and took shape, it became a vision. It became a vision that was shared with others, who then began to collectively take action on that vision, and the end result was a tangible, functional, beautiful, reality. It looks like this:

Dreams → Vision → Action → Reality

This is the process of vision, of moving things forward. By the way, this process is unique to humanity! I maintain that humans are the only creatures with vision! My dog does not have a *vision* for her life. I did not see her making a New Year's resolution list at the beginning of this year. She is not actively designing plans to build a tool that will allow her to open the cabinet where I keep her treats (cursed non-apposable paws!). Human beings, on the other hand, are created in the image of God and part of that *imago Deo* is the ability to dream, to refine that dream into a vision, to take action on that vision, and to see a new reality take shape.

The most striking example of this vision *process* that I know of is the story of the creation of the iPhone. Steve Jobs, the famed Apple CEO, had a vision of a "smart phone" – a computer with a touch screen that would fit in your pocket. Before the release of the iPhone there was nothing like it on the market, particularly the touch screen part. Jobs' vision was to remove all the buttons that had existed on the previous Apple products like iPod, and other products like Blackberry, and allow the user interface to be completely controlled by fingertip touch. This had never been done before on a device this small, and frankly not much at all. In fact, at the Apple event revealing the first iPhone, this new touch-screen technology shocked the audience present and subsequently the world. I would encourage you to find the video of the 2007 Apple Conference where Steve presents the iPhone and watch for the part where he introduces the scroll feature. When he "swipes" that screen with his finger to move the music albums up and down (a feature we now take for granted and use a thousand times a day), the gasps from the audience are *audible*. His vision becoming a tangible reality literally sucked the air out of the room.

Where *there is* no vision, the people perish:
But he that keeps the law, happy *is* he.
Proverbs 29:18

The word *vision* in this verse means "revelation" or "divine guidance". The context is that we should get our direction, our dreams, our vision, and our plans from the Lord.

The word *perish* does not necessarily mean death as we might be inclined to think; it more accurately is understood to mean "not caring about anything". It means to be empty, vacant, unoccupied; to have no direction and no potential. To have no vision for your life, your family, your work, your ministry, or your future is to perish in some real way.

When I think of this verse, I think of an empty building that I often pass in Metro Manila. Since I moved to the city over a decade ago, this 10+ story building has sat unfinished, empty, vacuous. What happens over time to a vacant building? A building with no purpose or use? It begins to decay. It begins to *perish*. It has lost its purpose, lost its potential, and therefore loses its glory and use. The same thing can happen to a person, a family, an organization, or a congregation. Vision and the actions that follow fight against this degradation around us.

Now that we've defined *vision*, we should dive in a bit deeper to get a better understanding of what vision is truly all about – how it plays out in the real work. And a great place to learn about the nuances of vision is from the story of Nehemiah.

Praying for the Vision

First of all, we see in the book of Nehemiah that he was a man of constant prayer. At the beginning of the book, he is working in the king's palace, and he received word that the walls of Jerusalem – his nation's chief city – are in ruins.

> So it was, when I heard these words, that I sat down and wept, and mourned *for many* days; I was fasting and praying before the God of heaven.
> Nehemiah 1:4

Nehemiah's first response to the tragedy is to fast and pray. His first response to a difficult situation is to spend time with God in prayer. Of note, he does not have a vision yet of what he should do. He is simply coming to the Lord. He doesn't even mention asking God for a vision or idea – He is just communing with his Lord.

Our primary source for vision must be the Lord. Nehemiah understood this. He comes to God for answers.

Nehemiah is also a man of Scripture, as we can see in his prayer:

Remember, I pray, the word that You commanded Your servant Moses, saying, '*If* you are unfaithful, I will scatter you among the nations; but *if* you return to Me, and keep My commandments and do them, though some of you were cast out to the farthest part of the heavens, *yet* I will gather them from there, and bring them to the place which I have chosen as a dwelling for My name.'
Nehemiah 1:8-10

This promise of the Lord that Nehemiah prays was originally given to Moses in Leviticus 26, and interestingly, in 2 Chronicles 6, King Solomon repeats this promise at the dedication of the new Temple. The promise is that if His wayward children will humble themselves and return to Him, that God will return them to Jerusalem.

The point is this - Nehemiah did not just become a man of prayer when he heard this bad news and realized the great need. He did not just start praying because he needed to ask God for something. He didn't write out his list for Santa Claus because it was December. No, he was a man of prayer already. He was a man of Scripture already. He spent time with the Lord regularly. And God led him when the time was at hand.

One of my favorite verses about vision is this:

Delight yourself also in the Lord,
And He shall give you the desires of your heart.
Psalm 37:4

What this verse says is that if we delight ourselves in God – spend time with Him, read His Word, pray and listen and follow Him, including spending time with other Spirit-filled believers in His church – then He will *replace* the desires in our life with new ones. In short, He will give us new vision for our life!

Waiting for the Vision

Nehemiah was the King's cupbearer. Literally, his job was to taste the drink before it was served to make sure it was safe. Poisoning royalty was a big thing at this time. So, a cupbearer was a person who was considered to be wise, honest, and trustworthy. Nehemiah was a man of recognized character and integrity.

This wise man sees the need of his people, prays to God, and then begins to form a vision of what he could do to help. A vision often forms in tandem with a burden to serve the Lord and meet a need. It did for Nehemiah.

He has this crazy idea in his head to go and help rebuild the wall of Jerusalem and secure the homeland of his people. Right. This was crazy, because #1 - he was the king's cupbearer – he could not exactly just walk out on his job. "Hey King, I can't come in to work for the next year or maybe two-ish because I'm going on a road trip to help rebuild a wall". No, it didn't work like that. And #2, it was crazy because the Jews had already tried to rebuild this wall about 40 years before this under the leadership of Ezra. King Artaxerxes had already stopped work on it:

> And I gave the command, and a search has been made, and it was found that this city in former times has revolted against kings, and rebellion and sedition have been fostered in it. There have also been mighty kings over Jerusalem, who have ruled over all *the region* beyond the River; and tax, tribute, and custom were paid to them. Now give the command to make these men cease, that this city may not be built until the command is given by me.
> Ezra 4:19-21

We learn further in the story that Nehemiah not only wants to leave his job to go and help rebuild the wall, he *also* wants to ask the king to *help* him with his grand vision. To do this, it was going to require patience, and a lot of it. In fact, Nehemiah had to wait a long time between his vision and his opportunity to ask the king. The month *Kislev,* when he first got the idea to go to Jerusalem, is equivalent to Nov-Dec on our calendar, and the month *Nisan* is equivalent to March-April. So, according to the text, Nehemiah had to wait four months to pursue this vision with the king! That is a lot of waiting!

Maybe God has given you a vision for your family, for your finances, for your children, for your ministry, or for your career. Are you patient enough to wait on God's timing? If you are like me, you want everything to happen immediately. Ask my wife - when I get an idea in my head, I am going to make that happen as soon as possible. I am learning to wait on the Lord and His timing.

Nehemiah did not even rush into the king's room right after he finished his prayer in chapter one and say "guess what?! I got a great idea!". No, he waited because he needed the right opportunity. And when the time was right, he presented his vision to the king, and the king responded:

> Then the king said to me (the queen also sitting beside him),
> "How long will your journey be? And when will you return?"
> So it pleased the king to send me; and I set him a time.
> Nehemiah 2:6

The king grants his request and makes it official by issuing letters making it a royal project of the Kingdom, with financial and military support! This was more than Nehemiah had asked for (and maybe more than he had prayed for)! Our God does things that like.

Not only was it more than he asked for concerning the wall, but Nehemiah was perhaps not fully aware that he was also helping to fulfill biblical prophecy about the coming Savior! This decree by the king is significant biblically, because it fulfilled a prophecy from the book of Daniel:

Know therefore and understand,
That from the going forth of the command
To restore and build Jerusalem
Until Messiah the Prince,
There shall be seven weeks and sixty-two weeks;
The street shall be built again, and the wall,
Even in troublesome times.
Daniel 9:25

This prophecy from Daniel was given in the year 539BC, almost 100 years before Nehemiah's time. The word "weeks" literally means a period of "seven", not actual weeks. It could read "there shall be 7 sevens" and "62 sevens", and *this* is best interpreted in the context of the book of Daniel as meaning *years*. So, 7 periods of 7 years is 49 years. And 62 periods of 7 years is 434 years. They total 476 years in the modern calendar and extended from 444 B.C. (Nehemiah) to A.D. 33, the year of the Triumphal Entry of Christ that we celebrate each year on Palm Sunday before Easter. [8]

So not only was Nehemiah a part of helping his people rebuild the wall, he was a critical part of bringing about the fulfillment of a prophecy about the life of Jesus Christ! His patience and trust in the Lord were rewarded with a task of eternal significance. And the same can be true for us! Many times, we may not even be aware of all that God is doing around, in, and through us – the major impact that our patience, action, prayers and decisions are having on the people, places, and things around us!

We must have patience when pursuing vision because we need the help of others to accomplish anything great for the Lord. We need counselors to speak into our lives. That takes time. We may need financial support. That takes time. We may need other people

---

[8] J. Dwight Pentecost, "Daniel," in *The Bible Knowledge Commentary: An Exposition of the Scriptures*, ed. J. F. Walvoord and R. B. Zuck, vol. 1 (Wheaton, IL: Victor Books, 1985), 1363.

to help us, encourage us. We may just need the right season of life. It all takes time. God may be waiting until the time is exactly right for the right things to happen, and we must be patient. Nehemiah had to wait and get the support he needed from those around him. While you are being patient, be faithful. That's exactly what Nehemiah did. He did not quit after one month and say, "forget this". He was waiting for the right moment – God's timing.

Clarifying the Vision

> So I came to Jerusalem and was there three days. Then I arose in the night, I and a few men with me; I told no one what my God had put in my heart to do at Jerusalem; nor was there any animal with me, except the one on which I rode. And I went out by night....
> Nehemiah 2:12-13a

I really love this part of Nehemiah's story. What is he doing here? He is already committed to his vision, his ultimate goal of rebuilding the wall. That has not changed. He has already been sent on his way and equipped by the king. But now he is refining, clarifying, and adding detail to what that will look like. Until this point, he had no real perception of what the wall looked like in its current state. He had heard stories and secondhand accounts, but there were no Google Map pictures for him to see, no TripAdvisor reviews to peruse. At this point, Nehemiah is in Jerusalem for the first time and he is now exploring, testing, and thinking about what he and his team will do.

Your initial vision will most likely be changed over time in some way. I'm sure Disney World looks different today than what Walt *first* dreamed up. I'm almost positive the first iPhone that was released was different than the original *first* draft. Refining vision is a part of the clarification process, and as we grow and learn, our vision grows with us – our drive expands, our expectation widens as we gain knowledge and experience – and we see the potential for more!

Announcing the Vision

An important part of realizing vision and making it workable and tangible is *announcing* it to the world, and that's exactly what Nehemiah did next. Up until this he had told no one of his plans:

> And the officials did not know where I had gone or what I had done; I had not yet told the Jews, the priests, the nobles, the officials, or the others who did the work.
> Nehemiah 2:16

Now pause for a moment and imagine the state of the people in Jerusalem at this time. Their hometown is destroyed. The wall – the very sign of peace and security– is completely in ruins. They had already tried to rebuild it a few years before and the king shut them down. And now there's some guy walking around the city at night with a notebook and a sparkle in his eye. My guess is that no one was excited, no one was impressed, no one had any vision yet of what was possible. Nehemiah's *job* was to cast the vision to them – to announce it and promote it. But like most leaders, he had an uphill battle to convince the people of this worthy cause.

> Then I said to them, "You see the distress that we *are* in, how Jerusalem *lies* waste, and its gates are burned with fire. Come and let us build the wall of Jerusalem, that we may no longer be a reproach."
> Nehemiah 2:17

First, Nehemiah acknowledges the reality. He admits that this will be a difficult task. Good leaders see not only in terms of the future, but in the reality of the present. If leaders do not acknowledge the current situation – good or bad - then their vision may just be a fantasy – something not grounded in reality.

If you told me that your vision for this year was to become the most successful *<fill in the blank>* ever – by year's end – I would very nicely challenge that "vision" and encourage you to bring it back down into orbit. We want to believe in big things, but we also have to believe in *realistic* big things.

The point is that you must see first your *reality*, and *then* decide not to stay in your reality, but move beyond it to a better future. Some people fail to remember where they are starting from and create goals that are unattainable.

On the other hand, some people make the mistake of looking at their reality and feeling "stuck" in their situation – they have a victim mentality. I just don't believe a Christian should think that way. I don't see this victim mentality in the Bible among God's people. Especially not with Nehemiah. Vision is the victim-mentality slayer! If you have a vision and are passionate about it, you will persevere through almost anything to bring it to fruition.

"Come let us build the wall...." - Nehemiah announces his vision with these words. He boldly, simply proclaims what it is that he has come to do. And perhaps, as soon as he said it, some people in the crowd groaned. Some people in the crowd thought "are you kidding me? This is what this guy gathered us here for? We already tried that man! Get a clue! It can't be done!"

But, as Nehemiah spoke to them, their negativity melted and was replaced by waves of hope and positive thoughts. They began to see what Nehemiah saw. They began to feel the potential of what could be. We don't have all the words that Nehemiah spoke to them – we have a summary and some of the words. But clearly, he inspired them as he cast the vision to them. This is why vision is so important in the life of an organization – it gives people a *reason* to be involved! Vision is the *why*. And the why changes everything.

And I told them of the hand of my God which had been good upon me, and also of the king's words that he had spoken to me.
Nehemiah 2:18

This verse is *very* important. Don't miss it. In casting the vision, Nehemiah gave them another reason to follow – he told them of "the hand of my God" – how God had helped him and the whole story up until this point. And the people began to see and realize that this was a special plan *of God*. What is a good way to get people involved in what the Lord wants you to do? Explain to them what the Lord has done in your heart and how He has led you to this point. Be vulnerable with people and they will respond to that openness!

For Nehemiah, a big part of clarifying his vision and gathering people around it was to announce it publicly – to talk about it openly. What vision are you holding onto that needs to be released out into the open so that it can breathe and find wings?

Teamwork for the Vision

So they said, "Let us rise up and build." Then they set their hands to *this* good *work*.
Nehemiah 2:18b

Nehemiah knew that he needed a team to accomplish this goal. And if you have a vision to do anything of any size, you will also need people to help you. If your goal is to brush your teeth every morning, you can handle that on your own. But God sized dreams require teams!

Teamwork: Coordination, Cooperation, and Commendation

Leaders who want to lead others into a vision – a preferred future - must do so in three areas that Nehemiah exemplifies: coordination, cooperation, and commendation.

Coordination

Every visionary who will actually accomplish something has to have some level of administrative ability. I do think that there are some creative geniuses out there with fantastically amazing visions that never see the light of day, because they are so unorganized and un-administratively geared. You must be *coordinated* if you will have vision and move it forward.

> Then Eliashib the high priest rose up with his brethren the priests and built the Sheep Gate; they consecrated it and hung its doors. They built as far as the Tower of the Hundred, *and* consecrated it, then as far as the Tower of Hananel. Next to *Eliashib* the men of Jericho built. And next to them Zaccur the son of Imri built.
> Nehemiah 3:1-2

In chapter three of the book of Nehemiah, he describes for us the building process that took place. And it shows an extremely high level of coordination. Phrases like "next to them" and "after him" occur twenty-eight times in chapter three! Every person had their specific place and their specific job. Nehemiah had done a lot of co-ordination and master planning!

Every smooth-running ministry, family, business, or venture worth mentioning each involves careful planning and preparation behind the scenes. One of the values in our ministries that I do my best to champion is *excellence*. Our worship service has a high standard of excellence, and most Sundays it hits the mark; and that's because there's a lot of planning and coordination. In staff meetings, we talk about things that need to be adjusted from the previous week. The band and worship leaders practice every week. We have the building cleaned every week. We prepare the slides and the notes ahead of time. Vision does not become reality by accident.

The same is true for a family. A well-behaved child who is obedient, kind, and courteous does not get that way on accident – I promise! They get that way through coordination! Through planning, execution (not *that* kind), correction, punishment, and reward – in what seems sometimes to be a never-ending cycle (can I get an amen, parents?). But the end results speak for themselves. The coordination pays off.

Nehemiah understood this principle of coordination, and he organized the people in painstaking detail. We know Nehemiah was a man of prayer – but he was also a man of action. He understood that prayer *alone* was not enough. There is a balance in the Christian life between the hand of God and the human responsibility that we have. A balance of prayer and work. Don't pray for something that you are not willing to work hard for!

Cooperation

"Let us arise and build". Almost everyone agreed to participate in the restoration of the wall. Unity in vision is so important. You cannot build anything of value without unity, without cooperation. You cannot strengthen your family without unity. You must have aligned values to achieve your vision for your marriage. You cannot have successful parent-child relationships without unity – cooperation around a common goal between each parent. You cannot build any business without cooperation of those around you. And you certainly cannot grow a ministry without it.

We understand that unity is needed. We pray for it. We seek it. Yet in spite of our best efforts to unify, there are always some detractors:

> Next to them the Tekoites made repairs; but their nobles did not put their shoulders to the work of their Lord.
> Nehemiah 3:5

Nehemiah does not complain or say why this group of "nobles" chose not to help, but these rulers, who lived outside the city walls most likely, would not join in the work. Maybe they thought it was below them, or simply unimportant - we don't know. Whatever the reason, Nehemiah did not allow a few people to distract or dissuade him in his task. Don't be discouraged as a leader if some people will not follow you; continue to build. Continue to champion unity and coordination among those who will follow.

Commendation

Encouragement is a powerful leadership tool. And if you are leading someone into a vision – whether your family, your kids, your co-workers, or your small group - you must be an encourager. Nehemiah was an encourager, because he took note of the great job everyone was doing and commented on it. God even tells us that we should be encouragers:

Therefore encourage one another and build one another up,
just as you are doing.
1 Thessalonians 5:11

All of us as believers are called to be encouragers. Even more so if you are a visionary - a leader moving people forward. I've heard it said that every leader should be a CEO –Chief Encouragement Officer. I think that's a good way to look at it.

To build a strong team for a strong vision, Nehemiah understood the importance of coordination, cooperation, and commendation. And he would need them, because he was about to have a fight on his hands.

Fighting for the Vision

But it so happened, when Sanballat heard that we were rebuilding the wall, that he was furious and very indignant, and mocked the Jews. And he spoke before his brethren and the army of Samaria, and said, "What are these feeble Jews doing? Will they fortify themselves? Will they offer sacrifices? Will

they complete it in a day? Will they revive the stones from the heaps of rubbish—*stones* that are burned?" Now Tobiah the Ammonite *was* beside him, and he said, "Whatever they build, if even a fox goes up *on it,* he will break down their stone wall."
Nehemiah 4:1-3

The enemies were rising up against the vision! And what was Nehemiah's response? Of course. The man of prayer prayed! In verse four he prays and asks God for help against their enemies. And then what? He steps out in faith...

So we built the wall, and the entire wall was joined together up to half its *height,* for the people had a mind to work.
Nehemiah 4:6

So we built the wall. I love that! Even in the middle of intense pressure and attacks, they prayed, and they kept moving! They were "all in". That the people "had a mind to work" literally means they had the *heart* or the *will* to complete it. In other words, they worked *enthusiastically.* They worked with passion! They worked with all their heart!

If you have a vision, and you move on it – you will find the naysayers quickly. Don't be discouraged. Be emboldened! I think this is why a sure calling, particularly in the Lord's work, is so important. A calling keeps you centered in the midst of battle, focused on the target. We have an Enemy that will attack and attempt to distract us, and we must respond in prayer and faith that moves forward. We must have a mind to work and continue building our wall.

As if external opposition was not enough, then Nehemiah faced some opposition from the inside:

Then Judah said, "The strength of the laborers is failing, and *there is* so much rubbish that we are not able to build the wall."
Nehemiah 4:10

The people working on the wall were so tired from day after day of work that they were literally stumbling, staggering, falling over from exhaustion. They were tired. They began complaining about the magnitude of the task – "there's so many rocks and debris to move". They started to believe that this plan was not going work. The task was too monumental! Not to mention, now they had enemies to worry about!

What did Nehemiah do in the midst of all of this opposition – internal *and* external naysayers? He kept fighting, he kept leading:

Therefore I positioned *men* behind the lower parts of the wall, at the openings; and I set the people according to their families, with their swords, their spears, and their bows. And I looked, and arose and said to the nobles, to the leaders, and to the rest of the people, "Do not be afraid of them. Remember the Lord, great and awesome, and fight for your brethren, your sons, your daughters, your wives, and your houses." And it happened, when our enemies heard that it was known to us, and *that* God had brought their plot to nothing, that all of us returned to the wall, everyone to his work.
Nehemiah 4:13-15

You *will* experience opposition to your vision. You will experience challengers from outside. You will experience discouragement - even coming from your own team! But have the courage to focus on the vision and push through! In the end, Nehemiah was victorious:

So the wall was finished on the twenty-fifth *day* of Elul, in fifty-two days. And it happened, when all our enemies heard *of it,* and all the nations around us saw *these things,* that they were very disheartened in their own eyes; for they perceived that this work was done by our God.
Nehemiah 6:15-16

Sources of Vision

I'd like to camp here for just a moment and reiterate the importance of the source of our vision. Nehemiah got his vision from the Lord – the ultimate source. To make sure we are also getting our vision from the Lord, we need to be aware of the potential sources of vision and ensure we choose the right one.

Source of Vision #1: Myself

Here is what Steve Jobs, former CEO of Apple, said about having ourselves as a source of vision:

"Your time is limited, so don't waste it living someone else's life. Don't be trapped by dogma - which is living with the results of other people's thinking. Don't let the noise of others' opinions drown out your own inner voice. And most important, have the courage to follow your heart and intuition."

"Follow your heart". What he is really saying is that you should not listen to anyone above your own self. You should think for yourself. Come to your own conclusions. The "opinions" of other people, in this way of thinking, are given a low priority. My own intuition and opinions are what count. Sounds pithy, maybe even wise. But, it's very dangerous.

Yet you can find example after example of this type of thinking in popular culture. And it sounds like this idea may have merit. It sounds like Steve could be on to something good. I mean, it's just dumb to go about blindly following someone, right? Instead we should be thinking intelligently about our decisions. It makes sense. But like every idea we encounter, we must view it through God's Word and what He says about it. Does God have anything to say about following your heart?

The heart *is* deceitful above all *things*,
And desperately wicked;

Who can know it?
Jeremiah 17:9

The Hebrew word for *heart* here means "inner man" - my inner thoughts, my desires, who I really am. God says that my heart is *deceitful* more than it is anything else. So deceitful that no one can understand how deceitful it is! So deceitful that it can deceive even me....

There is a way *that seems* right to a man,
But its end *is* the way of death.
Proverbs 14:12

So, because of the deceitfulness of my heart, I can follow a path that I feel is straight, correct, and right – but it is in reality a *sinful* path, a path leading to death and destruction. My heart can deceive me into thinking that I am going the right way when in reality I am going the wrong way.

We call this "justifying" our actions. It's easy to see wrongdoing in other people. It is harder to see it in yourself. You see this with sexual temptations – people justifying their sinful relationship to themselves. You see this in financial matters. A lot of people who steal have justified it in their minds first. I saw a news story this week, and the thief left a note that said, "sorry my kids are hungry". He has justified his wrong action, so that it seemed right to him to do it! Our hearts are deceitful – deceiving our own selves!

Sorry, Steve - if your source of vision for your life is just *you* – you are in danger of being deceived and going the wrong direction. I've counseled many, many people who made decisions – financial decisions, career decisions, school decisions – and the only person they consulted was themselves. And it ended badly.

Do you see a man wise in his own eyes?
There is more hope for a fool than for him.
Proverbs 26:12

Do you think you have all the answers? You don't! Do you think you can be your own source of vision and be successful? You will fail! So, we better move on and find a better source of vision for ourselves.

Source of Vision #2: Others

He who walks with wise *men* will be wise,
But the companion of fools will be destroyed.
Proverbs 13:20

This verse explains the principle that *influence has impact*. If you spend your time with wise people you will be *influenced* in that direction. Your vision will begin to be shaped in that direction – and you will end up yourself being wise, and mature, and godly in your decisions.

The opposite is also true. If your friends are all foolish, your life will be destroyed. What is a fool? A fool is someone who does not have wisdom, who does not care to listen to God's wisdom, and who goes about their own way. Those are not the friends and influences that you want as a source of vision. Don't ask your friend who cannot keep a job for career advice! Don't ask someone with huge relationship problems for marriage advice! Seems like common sense, but people do it every day.

Do not be deceived: "Evil company corrupts good habits."
1 Corinthians 15:33

You think you can be best friends with sinful, evil people living in sinful, wicked atmospheres, and still have a Godly, Christ centered vision for your life? Do not be deceived. The Bible has a lot to say about finding *good* sources to guide us in our lives and help us craft our vision:

Where *there is* no counsel, the people fall;
But in the multitude of counselors *there is* safety.
Proverbs 11:14

When you don't have any counsel from others, and you only listen to yourself, you will be brought down. You will not reach the goals God has for you. You will fall. But when you listen to the advice of many wise, godly people, you will find safety in your decisions. The word "safety" is the word for salvation or deliverance. The idea is that there are many, many wrong directions to go in our lives. You can choose many wrong, dangerous paths. For example, you can very quickly make the wrong financial decisions that have lasting negative impacts on your life. I have watched people give a lot of money to a business or venture when they were counseled *not* to do it by wise people. And they did it anyway. And they lost the money. There is *safety* in listening to wise people in our lives.

Without counsel plans fail,
but with many advisers they succeed.
Proverbs 15:22

What counselors are helping shape your vision?

Source of Vision #3: Jesus Christ

Jesus can (and should) be our source of vision through two primary ways that He has given us as gifts, as part of the abundant life that we have in Him: His Word and His Spirit.

The Word of Christ

Oh, how I love Your law!
It *is* my meditation all the day.
You, through Your commandments, make me wiser than my enemies;

For they *are* ever with me.
I have more understanding than all my teachers,
For Your testimonies *are* my meditation.
I understand more than the ancients,
Because I keep Your precepts.
Psalm 119:97-100

I love Psalm 119, because this chapter is God's commentary telling us what *God* thinks about *God's* Word. When God through His Word is your counselor, you are wiser than any of the enemies that are out to destroy you: Satan, sin, or evil people with wicked intentions. You are wiser! You are stronger! When God's Word is with you – meaning you know it, you have memorized it, and you are applying it – you have the *greatest* counselor the world has ever known at your side! You have more understanding than your teachers. When you are meditating on it – God's Word makes you wiser than the most intelligent, smartest people in the room – the people that *should* be teaching you! And last, when you follow God's Word, you understand more than those who are older than you. Wisdom and understanding – (read: vision!) – come from memorizing, meditating on, and following God's Word.

Your word *is* a lamp to my feet
And a light to my path.
Psalm 119:105

The Spirit of Christ

For as many as are led by the Spirit of God,
these are sons of God.
Romans 8:14

As Christians, we have the Spirit of God dwelling inside of us. An amazing truth! And we are told in this verse that the Spirit will lead us if we allow Him. He will be a source of vision for us. I don't need to look to myself for guidance, or try to follow someone else's dogma – I can look to Him.

> But he who is spiritual judges all things,
> yet he himself is *rightly* judged by no one
> 1 Corinthians 2:5

I can judge – or *evaluate* – all things through the Spirit of God in me. I can look at situations, pray about them, study God's Word, and be guided by His Spirit to the right decision. That's a pretty powerful place to be.

One indicator that I look for when I make decisions is peace. If I have peace about something after praying, counseling with people, and studying God's Word – then I am sure that I have God's answer. Jesus is the Prince of Peace – and through His Spirit He brings peace and direction to our decisions. Jesus is the ultimate source of vision for every believer, and we should rely on Him – His Word and His Spirit – as we craft our vision for our life.

Now, back to our original thought experiment at the opening of this chapter: does *vision* conflict with being *content*? It's a good question and one we need to wrestle with now.

What is contentment?

> Now godliness with contentment is great gain. For we brought nothing into *this* world, *and it is* certain we can carry nothing out. And having food and clothing, with these we shall be content.
> 1 Timothy 6:6-8

The word contentment means "satisfaction in one's circumstance or position in life". To be content is to be satisfied with whatever place you find yourself in, assuming your basic needs of food, clothing, and shelter are met. Anything on top of those essentials is just "icing on the cake" – not a requirement to be happy or satisfied.

So, what is it that keeps us so often from being content? For starters, we often look to other's situations around us and that makes us discontented, dissatisfied with our own lot. We see the money that our friend has, or the children that our neighbor has, or the job, or the intellect, and on and on, and we develop a desire to have more, achieve more. Comparison leads to discontentment. I think Americans struggle more with this than many other nationalities, because of America's affluence. I live and work in a developing nation, and I frequently travel to other developing nations and have many friends and co-laborers-in-Christ in these third world countries. And what I have learned is that living in an affluent society or being affluent does not ensure contentment. In fact, it may hinder contentment. Because when everyone around you is obtaining more and more wealth, bigger and more expensive toys, and growing their collection of material things – you cannot help but compare your situation to theirs. And if money does not buy happiness, it sure does give the impression of it. When I see the guy in the brand-new pickup truck pulling the brand-new bass boat down to the lake, there is a little part of me (and in any fisherman) that would love to be that guy. I compare myself to his situation, when in reality I know nothing about him! I have no idea what his life is like, what his relationship with the Lord is like, what is going on in his mind and heart – and yet I compare my external circumstance to his, and his seems to be preferential. And as we live in this environment day in and day out, we get caught in a cycle of constant comparison that changes the way we see *our* circumstance.

I should probably not write this. I may delete it before this is published. But here it goes. As a whole, we Americans are spoiled and entitled. There, I said it. I have been in conversations where people have complained to me about the size of the bedrooms in their home and how they needed a bigger house because of this– when most of the world's families live in studio-style one room dwelling, with multiple family members sharing the one sleeping space. My house in the Philippines does not have built-in closets, central air conditioning, or piped hot water. We have no front or back yard, and I don't have to guess what is generally going on in my neighbor's house be-cause I can hear every conversation through the open-air windows that are 12 feet apart from our house (also with open-air windows). Because of comparison, we often cannot be content until we have the extra square footage and a walk-in closet. I include myself in this, by the way. I am not trying to present myself as some sort of holier-than-thou person who is above all this. But what I have observed is that money does not buy contentment. Some of the most joyful, sat-isfied people I know live in places with no electricity, no running water, leaking roofs, and a dirt floor. And they serve the Lord with gladness and He meets their every need.

Contentment is only real if it would still remain after you stripped everything above basic needs away. The Bible says that if you have a relationship with the Lord and have food and clothes you can and should be content; that you don't need to compare your sit-uation to anyone else's. But we often search for more. And when we look past our basic needs for more, we are really looking for some-thing other than Jesus to satisfy us:

Let *your* conduct *be* without covetousness; *be* content with such things as you have. For He Himself has said, *"I will never leave you nor forsake you."* So we may boldly say: *"The Lord is my helper; I will not fear. What can man do to me?"*
Hebrews 13:5-6

Without covetousness in this verse means "free from the love of money". Meaning, we don't look to get more and more and more material things as the goal of our daily life. The reason we are work-ing should not be ultimately to buy more stuff. We are to be content with the food and clothing that we have. We are to be content with where we are materially. Why? Because the Lord is with us and He is our helper. Our satisfaction is found in Jesus. When we forget Him, and start looking other places, we lose our satisfaction.

But how does this biblical concept of contentment mesh with pursuing a vision of the future? If I am content, why would I work towards something else in the future? Why did Nehemiah even think about rebuilding the wall? Shouldn't these two concepts be mutually exclusive?

Contentment and Vision - Together

It is really not a question of either/or but of both/and. We don't need to choose between having contentment or having vision. We can have both, as long as they remain in balance. We have to look at the whole account of God's Word and realize that He gave us the doctrines of both contentment and vision, and He obviously wants us to have *both* in our lives. As in the other areas in this book, the problems occur when we are out of balance. The problems occur when we view the dynamic as a mutually exclusive choice – either/or.

First, contentment acts as a restrain on vision – a check and balance, if you will. A lack of contentment unleashes vision and drive to become something it should not be. When we are not satisfied in Christ, we feel the need to do more, prove more, achieve more at no end – we must always have "more". Think "work-a-holic" type situations.

I grew up a big NASCAR racing fan. I would watch almost every race on Sunday afternoon in-between Sunday morning and Sunday evening church services. I have distinct memories of sitting in the church parking lot, listening to the final laps of a race, and then racing in myself to the building to make it on time for the worship service. One of the most exciting types of racing to watch (or listen to!) is what they call "restrictor plate" racing. A restrictor plate or air restrictor is a device installed at the intake of an engine to limit its power.[9] In layman's terms, it's a metal plate with some holes in it, that when installed, prevents some airflow into the engine, thus reducing power and therefore speed. The main goal of a restrictor plate is to limit the cars from reaching speeds *above* 200mph. The

[9] https://en.wikipedia.org/wiki/Restrictor_plate

engines on these cars are so powerful, that if left unchecked on a large track like Daytona Speedway in Florida, the results would be really fast – and really dangerous. While the engine still operates as it should in a restrictor plate race, it's controlled for the environment that it's in.

In the same way, without contentment, the engine of vision is unrestrained. Contentment is the restrictor plate for vision. Left unchecked, vision and drive will leave much destruction in their wake. As an example from everyday life, a "workaholic" has very little contentment, by definition. Yes, they enjoy what they do and take pleasure in their work many times, but they are never satisfied. They are always looking for more, always feeling the need to achieve more. In short, their vision has lost its restrictor plate somewhere along the way.

King Solomon had something to say about this kind of person:

Unless the Lord builds the house,
They labor in vain who build it;
Unless the Lord guards the city,
The watchman stays awake in vain.
It is vain for you to rise up early,
To sit up late,
To eat the bread of sorrows;
For so He gives His beloved sleep.
Psalm 127:1-2

What this verse teaches is that there is a point of diminishing returns when it comes to our work, and this tipping point is Divinely appropriated. When we are not resting and content in Christ, we labor in vain. When we work without stopping, we are trying to build the house our self, and we are not trusting the Lord to take what we have worked for and multiply it. God's desire is for us to have periods of rest, periods of sabbath. When we ignore that, we violate His principles and His Word. It turns out that it is useless to work overly long hours at all. God will care for us, and thus, we should be able to work hard, and then rest contently.

Now please don't misunderstand. I do believe in hard work. God *also* says this:

> If anyone will not work, neither shall he eat. For we hear that there are some who walk among you in a disorderly manner, not working at all.
> 2 Thessalonians 3:10-11

> But if anyone does not provide for his own, and especially for those of his household, he has denied the faith and is worse than an unbeliever.
> 1 Timothy 5:8

God wants us to work hard – to run our engines at full capacity. But He also reminds us that we are running on the superspeedway called life, and we need to run with the restrictor plate of contentment in mind.

On the other side of the coin, a lack of vision makes contentment an idol. We can be tempted to use contentment as an excuse to avoid hard work. That's out of balance. God clearly wants us to have vision, to work toward goals, to pursue a better future. Vision is Godly – a part of godliness. God is the Creator; God has a vision and plan for your life. And to be like Him means to do the same – to have a vision. The key is the balance - to have this vision together with contentment. Vision acted upon from a heart of contentment is God's ideal for us.

Nehemiah needed to be content where he was and what he had before him – resting in his relationship with the Lord, while at the same time having a vision for a better future. This balance allowed him to move patiently, wisely, and carefully all throughout the process of rebuilding the wall of Jerusalem. If he had not been content, his vision would have been unrestrained and likely would have exploded in a blaze of glory. If he had no vision, he would never have left the king's palace.

Finding Your Divine Ideal

Finding the right balance of contentment and vision often involves a process of saying "yes" to a few select things and "no" to a lot more things. British Prime Minister Tony Blair said that "the art of leadership is saying 'no'." Warren Buffet, the American billionaire investor said, "The difference between successful people and very successful people is that very successful people say 'no' to almost everything." Steve Jobs said ""People think focus means saying 'yes' to the thing you've got to focus on. But that's not what it means at all. It means saying 'no' to the 100 other good ideas that there are." All of these leaders are speaking to the fact that you must first know what you are committed to, so that you can reject other opportunities efficiently. You must first know what you want to do, before you can know what you don't want to do.

This principle of focus, when applied to ministry, is even more critical. Because we are not dealing in financial gains or widgets, we are dealing with eternity.

You will struggle with ministry scale and impact until you learn to focus on what God made you to do - what I call your *Divine Ideal*.

Divine Ideal: More Opportunities Than Possible

One of the biggest challenges for servants of Christ is knowing which ministry opportunities to follow and which to avoid. If you are like me, you have more opportunities than you can possibly realistically engage in. Sometimes we engage in the wrong ministry because of the sheer volume of choices. When we were starting our first church plant, God opened the door for us to have access to a local elementary school. The principal, who was not a Christian, agreed to allow me to lead their daily faculty 'moral value' session. I was *sure* this was a great opportunity! How could it not be? So, once a week, I started leading their meetings and introduced some Bible topics. The problem - and what I did not understand at the beginning – was that none of the teachers wanted to be there - they were *forced* to be there by the principal. And they certainly didn't want to hear from me, a Baptist preacher. After a few weeks of that, *I* didn't want to be there, because none of them were responsive or engaging with me in any way. It was a tortuous few weeks. I was actually glad when that opportunity had run its course. It was just the wrong ministry opportunity. In the end, I was uncertain why I was even there. Have you ever felt like that? Have you ever been uncertain in what you were doing in your life and ministry? Uncertainty in ministry is not a fun place to be.

If you are a leader, it's even worse. Being uncertain as a ministry leader is like an airplane pilot with no real destination. He should have a plan, other people who are counting on him *assume* he has a plan, but really, he is just up there on a trip to nowhere. In ministry, being certain or being sure means not only knowing what you *want* to do, but more fully, knowing what you are *called* to do. If you are going to follow the right path, you must know that you have a *God* idea so that you can say no to other *good* ideas. You must learn to find and focus on your Divine Ideal.

When any of us in church leadership consider launching a new ministry, we often ask questions like "will this be effective?" or "will this connect?", or the most popular "will this be expensive?" (can I get an amen?). As a missionary pastor I ask that last questions a lot! Those are important questions so that we do not get out of touch with those we are most trying to impact. But are we asking spiritual questions to match our pragmatic questions? We must not only find good ideas. We must land on God ideas.

Experiments

Don't raise your hands, class, but how many of you have started new businesses or ministries only to see them fail? We all have. That's why I tell our team that everything is an experiment. We try this, it works. We try this, it fails. But regardless we learn and move forward. And that makes us not only *feel* better – it actually truly makes us better through shared, teachable moments. Sometimes failure is God's plan for our own growth and our own good. And that kind of experiment is good. Other times however, we miss the mark simply because we started off on a path that was not blessed. We engaged in something that was not God's intention. We are not experimenting inside of our calling; we've missed our calling altogether.

How can we know the difference? A wing and a prayer and go for it? See what sticks? There must be a better way. There must be a way that we can avoid wasting precious time and energy and focus on only the things that God wants us to be about. There must be a way to lock onto our Divine Ideal. There is. The secret is in the book of Psalms.

Delight yourself also in the Lord,
and He will give you the desires of your heart.
Psalm 37:4

The secret to finding God's idea is to first find God. The secret to fulfilling God's desire for your life and ministry is to delight in Him. The key to accomplishing for Christ is abiding in Christ. The secret to doing is being. The secret to finding your Divine Ideal is to focus on your Divine Maker.

Missed Opportunities?

Sometimes we are nervous about missing an opportunity, and that's why we try everything that comes our way. But missing opportunities *intentionally* often leads to greater results in the end. That's how God's Kingdom works. That's really how anything in leadership and progress works. Even Steve Jobs and Tony Blair understood this.

And they went through the region of Phrygia and Galatia, having been forbidden by the Holy Spirit to speak the word in
Asia. And when they had come up to Mysia, they attempted to
go into Bithynia, but the Spirit of Jesus did not allow them.
Acts 16:6-7

The Apostle Paul had a desire to take the gospel into Asia. He was
ready to go! How did he know not to take the gospel there? Why
wouldn't he want to stop there and preach? How could he miss this
opportunity? Because it wasn't God's idea. It was not Paul's Divine
Ideal. He delighted himself in the Lord. He listened to the Spirit. He
chose his ministry carefully. He understood what it means to delight
yourself in the Lord. By following Him, missed chances become
trails to greater opportunities. Seeming defeats transform into wonderful victories. Closed doors guide us to wide open ones.

Benefits of Clarity

The importance for each of us to know our Divine Ideal cannot
be overstated. The benefits of clarity around our vision are numer-
ous. By living your Divine Ideal, you will benefit yourself, your family, your church, and the world as the gospel is shared further and
faster. When you understand your Divine Ideal, you are no longer a
pilot flying aimlessly. You are a fighter pilot with a clear target and a
clarified mission to accomplish.

Let's learn to speak and live the truth with clarity and purpose.
Let's do more by perhaps doing less. Let's find our Divine Ideal and
say "no" to all the other good things. In doing that, God will be glori-
fied, His gospel will be proclaimed, and we will walk in a path of cer-
tainty.

Does God want you to have a vision and work hard to achieve it?
Yes! Does He want you to worry and lose sleep and be overly concerned about it? No! Does God want you to be content with where
you are and what you have? Yes! Does He want that contentment to
be your excuse to stay where you are? No. You are *already* a success

in Christ because of your status in Him. Be content. AT THE SAME TIME, He has saved you to serve – to do good works. Go serve! Go have a vision! Go accomplish something!

> And God *is* able to make all grace abound toward you, that you, always having all sufficiency in all *things,* may have an abundance for every good work.
> 2 Corinthians 9:8

This verse is a great way to end the chapter, because it summarizes the idea of balance between contentment and vision. Interestingly, the word for *all sufficiency* can also be translated *contentment* (as it is in 1 Timothy 6:6). What this means is that God in ALL His grace towards us, makes us completely content in ALL things in Him, so that we can go and serve Him – having vision and working hard - in every good work that He calls us to! We are content and we have vision to serve – at the same time. Balance.

Small Group Discussion Guide

After reading the chapter discuss the following questions below.

1) Read Proverbs 29:18
How would you define "vision"?
What does the word "perish" mean?

2) Read 1 Timothy 6:6-8
Discuss some things that keeps us from being content.
Where should our satisfaction come from?

3) What happens when we have a lack of <u>contentment</u> in our lives? Discuss the problems that can arise.

4) What happens when we have a lack of <u>vision</u> in our lives? Discuss the problems that can arise.

5) Which area do you need help balancing in your life - Vision or Contentment? How can you improve or change?

CHAPTER 6

The Balance of Boundaries and Freedom

We all crave freedom. We value freedom at the highest level. In almost every area of our life – We. Want. Freedom. I want freedom to make decisions for my family. I want freedom in how I lead and apply myself in my work. I want the freedom to follow the Lord and His calling on my life.

But it is important to understand that true freedom always comes with boundaries. If there are no boundaries present, it's not freedom, it's anarchy. Freedom disappears when boundaries disappear.

Imagine we visit your local zoo together. And there is a cage with an ostrich and beside it a cage with a cheetah. I may look at the ostrich, trapped in its cage, and think – "that poor animal – it has no freedom!". Now, imagine that the cages are removed, and the ostrich finds himself in the same enclosure with the cheetah. The walls are gone. The boundary is removed. The ostrich is free! Free to roam. But so is the cheetah. The ostrich only has the illusion of freedom now, because he is only free to go where the cheetah will allow him, and he will most likely soon meet his end.

In the same way, boundaries are a requirement for true freedom. Remove them, and you get a quasi-freedom that is no longer genuine. It may look like freedom, even feel like freedom for a time, but in the end, it leads to more captivity than the boundaries ever mandated.

This is true because you and I are not God (see chapter one) and we don't make the rules on what is and is not permissible. We don't even make the rules on what true freedom really is and how to experience it. True freedom as a human being comes from being in relationship to our Creator Jesus Christ. Apart from Him, we may feel like we have freedom to choose something else, but really, we are living with the illusion of freedom like the ostrich in the open, with the enemy ready to attack. God created the world, He created you and me, and He designed us to be in relationship with Him, walk with Him, and obey His commands. That is freedom defined for you and me. I can't just do whatever I want and call it freedom. But I can (hopefully) find a place in this world where I am allowed and able to do what God wants me to do. That is freedom.

True freedom is being who God made you to be and doing what He made you to do. Everything else is slavery.

Boundaries

There are good applications of boundaries and bad applications of boundaries all around us. The boundary of law and order, which in the United States is given by the Constitution and code of related laws and upheld by leaders and law enforcement, is a good boundary. For example, if we removed the specific boundary of the law dealing with right to life – laws that in general say someone cannot harm or injure another person or property without recourse - society would devolve into a place of revenge and anarchy. When used appropriately, this boundary protects life, property, and institutions that we hold dear. It promotes freedom in that it enables moral, honest citizens the opportunity to move about and live their lives in safety and security.

However, the same general boundary – the law – can be misappropriated and misused in ways that does not promote freedom, but instead limits it. The law unjustly applied to citizens creates a totalitarian state where no one is free to do anything, other than what the government gives them permission to do. Freedom disappears with the over-application of the boundary of laws.

In his book "Boundaries for Leaders", Henry Cloud writes that "good boundaries, both those that help us manage ourselves and lead others, always produce freedom, not control."[10] It is when we either fail to recognize good boundaries, or we recognize them and reject them, that we are in trouble. In our search for freedom, by throwing off God's divine boundaries, what we are doing is putting ourselves in the open with the cheetah. The cheetah is just as real as the boundaries, and when we seek to step outside those real boundaries, the real cheetah is there waiting.

Finding the Balance

There is a balance of accepting external boundaries in our life and simultaneously pursuing freedom – true freedom. This is a balance that we see played out in Scripture.

First, to find balance we can learn how to deal with unjust boundaries. There is a principle in Scripture that teaches us that we cannot allow unjust boundaries to prevent us from serving the Lord. The Apostles dealt with unjust boundaries – boundaries designed to thwart the Word of God – and they responded with force:

And when they had brought them, they set *them* before the council. And the high priest asked them, saying, "Did we not strictly command you not to teach in this name? And look, you have filled Jerusalem with your doctrine, and intend to bring this Man's blood on us!" But Peter and the *other* apostles answered and said: "We ought to obey God rather than men. Acts 5:27-29

---

[10] Henry Cloud, Boundaries for Leaders

This was a direct, forceful defiance against the authorities in charge. It was justified because the boundaries were unjust – they were not boundaries leading to true freedom, but boundaries designed to crush that freedom. Those kinds of boundaries can and should be justly refused.

On the other side of the coin, we cannot simply run the race of life however *we* deem best, removing whatever boundaries our opinion tells us are unjust, and setting up our own. The definition of freedom is not arbitrary. We must play by the rules. The Apostle Paul addresses this very subject:

> And also if anyone competes in athletics, he is not crowned unless he competes according to the rules.
> 2 Timothy 2:5

Paul is talking about running the Christian race, life in general, in his letter to Timothy. He is reminding Timothy of the powerful principle of boundaries. He is exhorting him that there are indeed some things that he *cannot* do, and some things that he *must* do. There are boundaries that are fixed that he must observe in order to run well.

If a runner in an Olympic race decides half-way through to start running outside the lines, taking shortcuts, running backwards, and skipping obstacles – he would be disqualified. Why? Because he is no longer truly running the race. He is ignoring the fixed boundaries. In the same way, there are many people who ignore God's boundaries in many areas of life. While they may appear to have freedom in the moment, in reality they are like the runner who is no longer participating in the race. And God is the one Who will judge us in the race of life – whether we ran according to His boundaries, or we did our own thing. Doing our own thing will not lead to victory and reward. In the end, it leads only to shame and regret.

This dynamic of freedom and boundaries plays itself out in several areas of life: our work, our families, our other relationships, and our ministries. Let's examine first the idea of boundaries as they relate to our occupations.

Area #1: Freedom and Boundaries in our Work

Imagine that you are starting a new job. You show up the first day, and the boss hands you a blank yellow legal pad and a pen, and shows you to your desk, which is bare other than a small company branded paper weight. All he says to you before he leaves is "good luck kid" and walks away. For a few moments you sit in silence wondering what just happened. There was no orientation, no SOP manuals to read, no nothing. You have no idea what your goals should be, what your task list should look like, or even what the company's goals for this quarter and this year are. While it seems like you have a blank slate and could do whatever you want – including taking a nap – in reality you have no freedom. You are stripped of your ability to be productive, because your boundaries have been removed.

Now, imagine a different scenario. This time you walk into your new job on the first day, and you are greeted (to use the term loosely) by your new boss with a 'huff', a side-eye, and a "well, I guess you will have to do" comment. The boss leads you to your desk, upon which are stacked several manuals that he instructs you to read through by lunchtime. As you take out a pen to start taking notes on his instructions, he rips it from your hands and shouts "we only use black ink in this office, by the way". Then he tells you that your lunchbreak will be from 11:13AM to 11:37AM, and you are required to drink two cups of water in the breakroom during lunch – a part of the mandatory "hydration policy" from corporate. Before you can ask him about what tasks you should focus on first, he hands you a "to do" list and says that he will give you a similar list every morning and expects it to be done exactly as instructed every day. No deviation. No opinions needed. Just assignments. You quickly realize that your freedom to be creative and work effectively has been completely removed in this environment – there are too many boundaries.

These two scenarios illustrate the importance of having the right balance of freedom and boundaries in the work that we do. While we do not want to work and lead in an environment where we are constantly micro-managed, we also have no desire to have a "job" with no clear goals, vision, or finish line. In short, we want to work in environments where we have the freedom *and* boundaries to do good work.

In order to find this balance, we must work in environments where the principle of delegation is understood. Without proper delegation, our workplaces will move to one of the two extremes.

Understanding Delegation

Webster defines *delegation* as "the act of giving power or authority to another person." Though it's simple to define, it's hard to do. In terms of practice, delegation is simultaneously one of the most referenced and least understood aspects of leadership. For workers in an organization with proper application of delegation - freedom and productivity abound. In places where delegation is incorrectly viewed as "command and control", the employees will inevitably feel boxed in and trapped by too many boundaries. Worse still, in a place where no delegation takes place, and everything lives in the boss' head – the absence of any clear direction creates nothing but chaos, confusion, and high turnover.

Understanding delegation is critical to maintaining balance between boundaries and freedom in our life and leadership. We all have tasks that we are responsible for, things that need to be accomplished. But are we required to be directly involved in every part of the task, in every decision along the way? What are the boundaries that limit our involvement, boundaries that give freedom? The answer is found in delegation.

I had a church member complain to me one time, because I was not "available" to go out *every* time on ministry activities at our church. I missed a few weeks of a certain regular outreach because of some other ministry responsibilities that were important. This member made a side comment to me and said, "well my pastor before (in a previous church) was always present on ministries like this even though he was very busy". For a moment, I was saddened that my actions had the appearance of disinterest or laziness. Did these observations mean I am not doing what I should be doing? Should I have made a way to be there for *all* of the meetings and activities? I pondered this. And then I realized that there was no need to be alarmed. Had I made a leadership miscalculation? Not at all (in this case at least!). In fact, I think that it's a bad sign when the pastor does *everything* in a church. It's a bad sign when the pastor shows up for every single activity in every department. That's a sign that he is not developing leaders, not equipping the saints, and not growing the church. A pastor that can do everything that needs to be done and does it, leaves no room for anyone else to serve. I know of a pastor who has been serving in a ministry for over fifteen years, and he is very busy right before the worship service on Sundays, folding all the bulletins to hand out that morning! Surely, someone else would have been honored to help out with that task. Surely, some simple delegation could have opened an opportunity of service for someone else.

Refusing to Delegate

The danger of refusing to delegate is two-fold. First, it prevents the leader from engaging in what only he can engage in, what he is called to do, and what must be done. And secondly, it prevents others from serving in capacities that perhaps *they* are called too.

Take a cue from the Apostles and how they led and administrated in the early church:

Therefore, brethren, seek out from among you seven men of good reputation, full of the Holy Spirit and wisdom, whom we may appoint over this business; but we will give ourselves continually to prayer and to the ministry of the word."
Acts 6:3-4

You and I must learn to delegate if we will be productive, and if we will provide opportunities for others under our leadership to grow. Ask yourself right now – 'where am I not delegating that I could be? Is that abdication preventing me from being productive? Is it preventing someone else from serving?' These are eye-opening questions that can help us find where we are either setting up the wrong boundaries (by preventing someone else from being involved in our work), or eliminating boundaries that should be there (we should be saying "no" to things that others could do). Both of these extremes limit freedom and harm productivity. That's why God has something to say about delegation and its importance.

The first recorded example of delegation in the Bible is in Exodus:

> And so it was, on the next day, that Moses sat to judge the people; and the people stood before Moses from morning until evening. So when Moses' father-in-law saw all that he did for the people, he said, "What *is* this thing that you are doing for the people? Why do you alone sit, and all the people stand before you from morning until evening?" And Moses said to his father-in-law, "Because the people come to me to inquire of God. [16] When they have a difficulty, they come to me, and I judge between one and another; and I make known the statutes of God and His laws." So Moses' father-in-law said to him, "The thing that you do *is* not good. Both you and these people who *are* with you will surely wear yourselves out. For this thing *is* too much for you; you are not able to perform it by yourself. Listen now to my voice; I will give you counsel, and God will be with you: Stand before God for the people, so that you may bring the difficulties to God. And you shall teach them the statutes and the laws, and show them the way in which they must walk and the work they must do. Moreover you shall select from all the people able men, such as fear God, men of truth, hating covetousness; and place *such* over them *to be* rulers of thousands, rulers of hundreds, rulers of fifties,

and rulers of tens. And let them judge the people at all times. Then it will be *that* every great matter they shall bring to you, but every small matter they themselves shall judge.
Exodus 18:13-23

In leading the children of Israel, Moses was wearing himself out. Oh, he had good intentions. He had the right heart. He was even obedient as far as the responsibility goes – he was trying to do the job the Lord had given him to do. But he was going about it in the wrong way. He did not have the proper boundaries setup, and as a result, instead of freedom all he was experiencing was slavery to the task. His father-in-law, Jethro, saw this glaring problem, and gave him some very specific advice. His step by step instructions regarding delegation are as relevant today as when they were first given.

Jethro's Rules of Delegation

Rule #1: Realize that overworking leads ultimately to failure

The thing that you do is not good. Both you and these people who are with you will surely wear yourselves out. For this thing is too much for you; you are not able to perform it by yourself.

Jethro labeled Moses' lack of boundaries as "not good". I think that's a pretty cut-and-dry assessment. What we have to understand is that while God has called us to good works, He has not built us as machines who perform tasks non-stop, with no help, with no break. Removing the boundaries of rest, reflection, and relationships does not secure more freedom for our lives; it only brings exhaustion and a law of diminishing returns on our productivity. If God had created us to be robots, working 24/7 without food and water, then we could accomplish much more than we do. If God had given me a computer instead of a brain, perhaps it could write and think and calculate faster and for longer periods of time – I could write a book a day probably! But that's not reality. That's not life inside the boundaries.

And that's not true freedom – being who God made you to be and doing what He made you to do.

Rule #2: Remember that you have a Divine Ideal

Stand before God for the people, so that you may bring the difficulties to God. And you shall teach them the statutes and the laws, and show them the way in which they must walk and the work they must do

God had specifically called Moses to the job of teaching the people God's truth and showing them how to apply it to their lives. But because he was busy making every little odd and end decision that the people brought to him, he was missing out on the big picture. Not only will refusing to delegate and involve other people leave you tired, it will also leave you missing the mark on your calling. We talked about our Divine Ideal earlier in this book; delegation is a big part of staying true to God's purpose for our lives.

Good delegation is also how others can find and live their Divine Ideal as well. Being unwilling to allow others to join you in your calling often prevents them from actualizing their own. Imagine how many leaders Moses had around him that were just sitting in the wings thinking, "you know, I could help him with this if he would just let me". How many people do we have around us that are just waiting – even anticipating – when they may be asked to serve? And the strange beauty of it is that some of the things that other people love to do, are the things that I dread doing. By delegating to them, I improve their life by giving them things to do that they love, while simultaneously removing some drudgery off my plate. A win-win!

Rule #3: Recruit select leaders to serve with you

Moreover you shall select from all the people able men, such as fear God, men of truth, hating covetousness; and place such over them to be rulers of thousands, rulers of hundreds, rulers of fifties, and rulers of tens

Next, Jethro instructs Moses to choose carefully who will serve with him. Jethro advised him to choose the *able* men – ones with excellence, strength, and ability. One of the things that drives me crazy in organizations is the "warm body principle". Leaders get it into their minds that as long as someone is breathing and has a desire to participate – they will be good for the job. That could not be further from the truth!

One of THE MOST important decisions that determines the success of a leader is choosing the people who will serve with them. I have determined, through observation guided by my experience, that my successes as a leader are largely due to the people that I've surrounded myself with and how I have led and mentored those people. Leadership is leading people, and great visions require great teams.

When I select people to serve with me on various teams, whether they are reporting directly or indirectly to me, I always follow the rule of "The Three C's of Team Selection". The Three C's are: character, chemistry, and competence.

Character

Character is who you are when no one is looking. *And* character is who you are when everyone is looking, or anyone is looking, or just one person is looking, or just your enemies are looking, or just your spouse and kids are looking. Character is who you really are.

Character is choosing to do the right thing all the time, every time. Those are the kinds of people that I want to work with, towing the line with me, serving alongside of me, and yes, taking directions and carrying out the vision.

"A big man is one who makes us feel bigger when we are with him" - John Maxwell. I like that quote. While it doesn't encapsulate everything about character, you can feel what he means. People with character are genuine, and their genuineness spills over into their steadfastness, their demeanor, and their integrity.

Chemistry

Chemistry is that innate ability to get along with others; to play nicely; to have emotional intelligence. Chemistry is crucial, because we must get *along* before we can get *moving.*

In my experience, chemistry is something that you *experience* with others. It is the integration between two or more people of the combination of words, body language, tone of voice, facial expressions, and attitude. But we don't consciously calculate all of those things and add them up like a math problem. We experience them with other people. We *feel* chemistry.

When I interview people to join my team, at some point in the process I normally invite them to dinner with *their* spouse and *my* wife. I learned this interview technique from Dave Ramsey in his wonderful book *EntreLeadership*. I apply it for two reasons: one, I want to see their interaction with other people in a social environment, and two, I want my wife to get a "feel" for the chemistry between all of us. There are decisions that have gone the other way, deals that have not been made, and paths that were not taken, all because my wife had a strange *feeling* about the chemistry with the other person.

There are people that I have not offered jobs too who were well qualified and honest, upstanding individuals. The reason I did not offer the job is because there was something in the chemistry that was not right. I literally imagined having to come to work and see this person every single day, and I knew that it would be a bad decision for them and for me. While it may seem "touchy feely" to some, I hope that I've at least made you think about what an important factor chemistry is when choosing team members.

Having the right chemistry helps in stressful situations that come up in any organization. If everyone relates on basically the same wavelength, difficult problems can be handled efficiently, and everyone can move on. Without chemistry, the slightest storm can rock the whole organizational boat.

Competence

The hard truth is that some people are just not made to be leaders. Some people are not comfortable making decisions, moving things forward, and taking risks. You must be sure that the people you delegate to are, as Jethro advised, able to do the job.

We must remember that people are gifted to perform specific tasks, not EVERY task! A person may have great character and really good chemistry with everyone in the office, but if they are not competent administratively, don't hire them to be the administrator! And yet, these sorts of hires happen all the time.

As believers, particularly when hiring in a ministry setting, we need to keep in mind spiritual gifts as taught in 1 Corinthians 12. While it is true that we can work to improve ourselves (2 Tim 2:15), in my estimation, we cannot improve what is not already there.

The main thing to remember with the "The Three C's of Team Selection" is that they must all be present in a person in order for you to confidently delegate to them. If one of the three is missing, disaster awaits. Jethro cautioned Moses to be careful of who he selected for leadership, because those selections would impact the results that Moses was responsible for. We must select the right people as stewards of the vision.

Rule #4: Let these leaders lead

And let them judge the people at all times.

Once you select the right people, you must allow them to work! This is a biblical example of and a model for delegation. The worst thing that a leader can do with a team member is to put them in a position, and then micro-manage them to the point where the leader is the one still doing the work. If a leader is not willing to let go of some of the process, they are not truly delegating (and maybe not even leading).

One key to letting go and not micro-managing is learning to delegate results *not* actions. If I delegate every single action that needs to be taken on a given project, and how and when it should be taken, then I might as well just do it myself and save everyone the trouble. But if instead I delegate the end result – the final *what* - and allow the team member to choose the *how*, *when*, and *where* – then I am on my way to effective delegation and dynamic leadership.

As a final thought to sum up this section on boundaries in our work - when delegating and letting leaders lead, there is a balance that must be found between freedom and boundaries. There is the need to let go and the simultaneous need to hold on. If I completely turn loose of the outcome of the assignment, then I have abdicated my leadership. If I hold on too tightly to the process, I am not really leading anything or anyone. Striking this balance between too much control and too little is the art of delegation. And thoughtful delegation leads to brilliant outcomes in our work and leadership.

Area #2: Freedom and Boundaries in Identity

The current climate says that traditional boundaries for identity, sexuality, and relationships in general should be removed. These traditional ideas, it is thought, limit freedom of expression and define a person with unfair social norms. In short, the argument says that societal boundaries are limiting personal freedom. In fact, just the opposite is true. The boundaries that God has set in place in the realms of biology, sexuality, and human interaction are there for a reason – to provide *ultimate* freedom and purpose in our lives. In short, we were created to live in certain relational ways, and when we do, we are the freest we could possibly be – free to live at our highest possible zenith.

I remember taking a sociology class as a freshman in college. It was part of the gen-ed requirement, not something I was particularly interested in. It was a stimulating class, and I learned some helpful things, but one idea in particular that I recall has stuck with me. The thought presented by our professor was that children do not choose their own gender specific toys as infants and toddlers, but rather these gender specific toys are forced on them by societal norms. For example, a boy does not *choose* to play with guns and swords and army men, but rather his parents or authority figures unwittingly forced these toys on the boy in order to confirm to societal norms, and thus it becomes his reality. The argument was the same for little girls – they did not choose to play with baby dolls and dress up like princesses; it is in fact society that forces these norms on them for better or for worse. In short, society is setting up boundaries limiting true freedom. Is this true? It seems plausible, maybe even possible.

Have you ever seen a little girl caring for a baby doll as if it was her real firstborn? Of course, someone could have forced the baby doll on her. Perhaps. But they could not force her, or even teach her, to treat the baby as she does. And in many of these cases the little girl has no younger siblings and has not observed a routine, daily pattern of infant care. When you see this scenario played out the only thing that you can do is smile because you realize that this is *nature* not nurture.

One of the arguments of sociologists is that you can nurture a child out of the traditional gender roles that they are forced to participate in by society. For example, you can give a boy baby dolls, dresses, high heels, and jewelry to play with– and he will *eventually* desire those things. But recent studies have shown this not to be true. Psychologists Dr Brenda Todd and Sara Thommessen from City University London conducted a research study with infants aged nine months to thirty-two months[11]. The researchers concluded that "the finding of sex differences in toy choice prior to the age at which a gendered identity is usually demonstrated is consistent with biological explanations of toy preference." In other words, boys choose boy toys no matter what, even at a very early age – almost like it is in their nature. Imagine that. But, the only study that we need to back this up is our own experience. What our own observations prove to

---

[11] https://digest.bps.org.uk/2016/06/03/infants-show-a-preference-for-toys-that-match-their-gender-before-they-know-what-gender-is/

us is that the boundaries of traditional society are not man-made - but Divine. They are not nurtured. They are natural. And what these natural boundaries bring is freedom. They bring the freedom of living life in relation to other people as God has designed.

Area #3: Freedom and Boundaries in Marriage

God has created us with differences. Those differences are boundaries that bring the freedoms of love, joy, and happiness into our relationships with one another. The words of Jesus affirm this:

But from the beginning of the creation,
God *'made them male and female.'*
Mark 10:6

The boundaries of male and female – the fact that I am a man and my wife is a woman – do not bring limits. They bring freedom. God is not in the business of enslaving people. Satan is. The Bible very clearly says throughout its pages that sin enslaves, and Christ frees. In speaking of Christian liberty, Paul writes:

Stand fast therefore in the liberty by which Christ has made us free, and do not be entangled again with a yoke of bondage.
Galatians 5:1

This verse is not to be applied only to spiritual activity, but to our whole lives. Because Christ has delivered us from the power of sin – fear, destruction, chaos, and death – we are free to live for Him and follow Him – we are more than conquerors. We are free to see and live inside our God-given boundaries. This is especially true in our marriages.

Boundaries in marriage are both positive and negative. There are things that I must do as a husband – positive boundaries. And there are things that I must not do – the negative boundaries. And likewise, the same is true for my wife. As each of us understands these boundaries and abides inside them, we have the freedom to love each other as God intended. It is when spouses step outside those boundary markers – either positive or negative – that they are losing their freedom to be who they should and could be. As Henry Cloud says, "boundaries help define the freedom we have and the freedom we do not have". [12]

Love can only exist inside proper boundaries. When we step outside those boundaries, we are no longer free to love. If one person is controlling another in some way, that's not love. If one person is ignoring a person in one way or another, that's not love. They are outside their boundaries and have lost the freedom, the ability, to show love. When we choose to ignore the boundaries that God has put in place in search of something better, we do not find more freedom. We lose it altogether. True freedom is found in knowing and observing the boundaries for us that God has put in place. The Bible has many things to say about marriage, and while this is not a relationship book, I hope this section has sparked your mind to study God's Word more on the subject of marriage and the boundaries and freedoms that God has put in place for you and your spouse.

Area #4: Freedom and Boundaries in Relation to God

People outside the Christian faith view belief in Jesus Christ as limiting – a religious structure of rules and negatives to avoid that takes all the freedom out of life. These same people attempt to live their life "to the fullest" by removing the boundary of a relationship with God. In reality what they're doing is removing the only boundary that can bring them true freedom.

Light is frequently used in the Bible to describe the Christian life. The Bible says that Jesus is the light of life, that Christians are to be a light to the world, that God himself is light, and that the Word of God is a light unto our path of life. Have you ever tried to move through a dark room where there was not one trace of light any-

---

[12] Henry Cloud, Boundaries for Marriage, 24

where? Do you have more freedom to move around in the dark than if the room was flooded with light? The answer is obvious. The light brings freedom. Yet many people reject the light of Jesus Christ and in so doing find themselves in confusing darkness that limits their movement.

We can think of boundaries like fences along a property. Landowners often erect a fence along the border of their property to clearly mark where the property begins and ends. Jesus said ""I am the way, the truth, and the life. No one comes to the Father except through Me" (John 14:6). In other words, Jesus said that He Himself is the boundary line. He is the only way to God. He is the only Way to true freedom. The boundaries that create the road provide the only path to freedom. We who trust in Jesus as the Way experience the freedom of life on the path to God. The "boundary" of a certain path does not limit life or freedom, but in reality, allows us to connect with the God of reality and thereby transcend our own selves. We are not walking in darkness, bound by our physical life, problems, sins, or difficulties around us. We transcend all of that by being in relationship with the God Who is the light of this world and Who defines reality. We live for a higher purpose – we live for Him.

Conclusion

The interplay of boundaries and freedom, and its impact on the intricate details of our lives and relationships, is inescapable. God has designed the world with certain rules, with a certain order, with certain boundaries. And because He is good, He has designed those boundaries not to bring slavery or difficulty, but to bring freedom. It is when God's boundaries are questioned instead of accepted, that sin enters and freedom vanishes. The first time God's boundaries were questioned was in the Garden of Eden. When Adam and Eve were in the garden, God gave them one rule: do not eat of the tree of the knowledge of good and evil.

Then the Lord God took the man and put him in the garden of
Eden to tend and keep it. And the Lord God commanded the
man, saying, "Of every tree of the garden you may freely eat;
but of the tree of the knowledge of good and evil you shall not
eat, for in the day that you eat of it you shall surely die."
Genesis 2:15

That is a restricting rule by any measure. It is a boundary. But for
Adam and Eve, God said it, so they did not question it. They trusted
God, and that boundary actually enabled them to have and maintain
all the freedom they could ever want. They were in the freest possible state in the freest possible place of any human beings that have
ever lived.

Now the serpent was more cunning than any beast of the field
which the Lord God had made. And he said to the woman,
"Has God indeed said, 'You shall not eat of every tree of the
garden'?" And the woman said to the serpent, "We may eat
the fruit of the trees of the garden; but of the fruit of the tree
which *is* in the midst of the garden, God has said, 'You shall
not eat it, nor shall you touch it, lest you die.' " Then the serpent said to the woman, "You will not surely die. For God
knows that in the day you eat of it your eyes will be opened,
and you will be like God, knowing good and evil." So when the
woman saw that the tree *was* good for food, that it *was* pleasant to the eyes, and a tree desirable to make *one* wise, she took
of its fruit and ate. She also gave to her husband with her, and
he ate.
Genesis 3:1-6

Satan challenges God's Word here with a direct subtilty. "Did
God *really* say?" Here Satan introduces, for the first time in recorded
history the idea that God's Word is open to our scrutiny and challenge. Before that, Adam and Eve rightly accepted God's Word as
being True and Good. Interestingly, Satan did not use "LORD God"

(Yahweh-Elohim) as the name for God here. That would have been too personal for Eve and may have reminded her of her good relationship with God. Instead, he used "God" (Elohim), making God a little bit more distant, not as personal, not as relational. Eve falls for Satan's deception, and begins to question God's Word in her heart. As she questions God's Word, she replies to Satan that God had said "Nor shall you touch it" as part of His instructions. God never said such a thing to Eve. Eve was now twisting God's Word, whether she realized it or not, and it made God seem harsh and unforgiving. (i.e. – "one little mistake and you will be killed"). Then Satan brings the attack to the forefront: "you will not surely die". This is no longer subtle. Satan is bringing a full attack on God's Word now that he has Eve's attention. Interestingly, Satan is calling into question God's ability and plan to judge the world – divine judgement. He questions God's power. He is prideful even when trying to deceive others.

Finally, in verse five, God's goodness is attacked. Satan convinces Eve that God does not have her best interests in mind, and that He is hiding something good from her. Eve is convinced that the boundary God has placed is not there for her prosperity and well-being but for her limitation and restriction. The boundary, Eve is convinced, is limiting her freedom. So, Eve ate of the fruit, she gave it to Adam, and they sinned by disobeying the Word of God. And they unleashed the power of sin to bring bondage and darkness upon mankind.

From the very first man and woman up to the present day, we as human beings have struggled with the balance of boundaries and freedom. We have a sinful tendency to want to look beyond the Lord and see for ourselves if there might be something better. The closer we grow to Christ the more we understand that to stay within His boundaries is the best way – the only way – to experience freedom in every area of our life.

Small Group Discussion Guide

After reading the chapter discuss the following questions below.

1) How would you define true freedom?

2) Read Acts 5:27-29
Why were the actions of the Apostles justified here?
When else is it okay to challenge boundaries?

3) Read Psalm 37:4
How can you find your Divine Ideal?

4) Review "Jethro's Rules of Delegation"
How can you apply these to your life and ministry?
How can delegation help you achieve balance?

5) What are the "good boundaries" that you most often challenge?
How can you learn to trust the Lord more in this area?

CHAPTER 7

The Balance of Grace and Truth

Grace and truth - two areas that sometimes seem to cancel each other out in our lives instead of existing harmoniously. It seems that we cannot possibly have both of these at the same time – grace *and* truth? Yeah, I'll get back to you on that. And yet, it *is* possible, through Him.

And the Word became flesh and dwelt among us, and we beheld His glory, the glory as of the only begotten of the Father, full of grace and truth.
John 1:14

Let not mercy and truth forsake you;
Bind them around your neck,
Write them on the tablet of your heart,
And so find favor and high esteem
In the sight of God and man.
Proverbs 3:3-4

We see in these two passages the reality and the calling to have grace and truth be a part of our lives at all times. In John, we learn that Jesus is full of both grace and truth, and in Proverbs we are reminded that God wants *us* to strive for these in our own lives. So, we are going to look at these two pillars of character – grace and truth – and find out how to live them out in balance in our lives. First, we need to define the terms.

What is truth?

> Jesus answered, "You say *rightly* that I am a king. For this cause I was born, and for this cause I have come into the world, that I should bear witness to the truth. Everyone who is of the truth hears My voice." Pilate said to Him, "What is truth?"
> John 18:37-38

Pilate was asking a cynical or sarcastic question here by saying "what is truth?". You can imagine a wry grin breaking across his face as he says it, as if he knows well and good that there is no real answer. As a leader in the ruthless Roman Empire, he had seen too much, done too much, to believe that there was ever one right answer, one solitary view corresponding completely to reality. What he really meant was, "look around at all the chaos and confusion and evil and death. Is there really such a thing as truth?"

Truth: *the property of being in accord with fact or reality*

For something to be true is has to be *real*. It has to conform to reality, by definition. Sometimes we think that things are true, but they are not in line with reality, so by definition they are not really true. We call that being deceived. When Eve was deceived by Satan, he tempted her and she believed a lie – in other words, she *thought* what she heard was the truth – but it was not.

As a magician, I often use the perception of reality to my advantage.[13] Not to get too in-depth (a magician never reveals his secrets), but magicians often use "sleight-of-hand" to make things appear one way, when in reality they are not. For the trick to be successful, it is not important what the reality *actually* is at any given moment, but what the spectator's *perception* of reality is. In the same way, Satan never alters the truth – truth is unchanging. He alters our perception of the truth through lies, doubts, and deception.

There are two very big statements the Bible makes about truth: Jesus is Truth, and the Bible is Truth.

Jesus is Truth

Jesus said to him, "I am the way, the truth, and the life. No one comes to the Father except through Me.
John 14:6

Jesus Himself said that He *is* the truth – meaning, He embodies truth - everything about Him conforms to reality! I think one of the greatest things about meeting and knowing Jesus is that He defines reality. If you are a believer in Jesus Christ, you know that you have heard the truth – indeed, you know the One Who is the truth! You know the truth about creation because He is the Creator; you know the truth about yourself because He is your Savior; and you know the truth about eternity because He is the eternal King.

The Bible is Truth

Sanctify them by Your truth. Your word is truth.
John 17:17

---

[13] For more information on Honest Deceiver Ministries visit www.honestdeceiver.org

The Word of God – the Bible – *is* truth. Everything it teaches, everything it says - conforms to reality. What God's Word tells us about the universe, about ourselves, about the beginning of time, about the end of time, about relationships, about sin, about love, about sex, about children, about justice, about balance – ALL of this and more conforms to reality. And if you base your life on it, you are basing your life on truth – what is real.

What is truth? Truth is reality, and reality is Jesus Christ and His Word. Or put another way, God in His person and in His Word defines truth and reality.

What is grace?

Looking back at the two verses at the beginning of this chapter, the word *grace* in John 1:14 gives the same idea as the word *mercy* in Proverbs 3:3.

Grace – *charis* – kindness, favor
Mercy – *hesed* – goodness, kindness, favor

For both of these words, *charis* and *hesed*, the overarching idea is goodness and kindness towards others. At least in these two passages, they are basically the same word.[14]

The grace and mercy of God is that quality of His by which He keeps His promises to us. It is His loyalty, His devotion, His loyal love. Grace is showing kindness and favor to someone who does not deserve it – which is what God does for all of us. And it is what He calls us to do for others. When we deal with someone *graciously*, it means we are treating them not how they may *deserve* to be treated, but in a good and kind way according to grace, regardless of their actions or words towards us.

---

[14] The concept of the Hebrew *hesed* is quite nuanced and outside the scope of this book

We know grace by experience, because when we receive it, it makes us feel grateful. It makes us feel like we owe something back. Have you ever had anyone pay for something for you? Maybe they bought your meal at a restaurant when you were not expecting it? I can remember going to a very nice restaurant with some friends, and at the end they said that they would pay for everything. I was thankful, and also very grateful – so grateful that I wanted to do something for them in return. Grace creates a bond, an indebtedness between people. Not a bond of slavery, but a bond of love. That's the love that grace creates. The Bible says that we love Him because He first loved us. (1 John 4:19). That's God's love, God's grace – the grace that we should show to others.

Grace and Truth Together

Let's look again at Proverbs 3:3-4:

Let not mercy and truth forsake you;
Bind them around your neck,
Write them on the tablet of your heart,
And so find favor and high esteem
In the sight of God and man.
Proverbs 3:3-4

In other words, grace and truth should be always with you, like a necklace that you would wear. They should be – figuratively of course – written on your heart. They should be a part of who you are – a part of your character. Both of them. Not one or the other. Both. At the same time. *Balanced.* Interwoven. Literally, a part of each other as they are a part of you. Inseparable. You get the idea. This is not an either/or choice. It's not that we should have at least one of them at all times. We should live our lives with both of them at full measure at all times. And if we do this, we will have favor and a good reputation - with God *and* other people!

The problems occur when we make a binary choice and choose one over the other. Sometimes we choose one over the other in a moment, with little thought. Think about the last time you had a heated argument with a family member. It was probably full of truth, but not much grace! Or think about the last time you didn't want to hurt someone's feelings, so you really did not give them the reality of what you really thought and were just kind to them - in place of the truth. In those moments, we are failing to live the balance that God wants us to have. When we remove either truth or grace from our lives, we are failing to represent Christ fully to those around us, and worse, we may even be giving a false picture of who we are in Him, and Who He is to us.

Sometimes we deceive ourselves in choosing either grace or truth - one over the other - *permanently*. I have heard people say things like "well I just speak my mind", or "I just don't have any mercy", or "I just don't want to be too harsh and unkind with them". What they are telling themselves is that they are simply not capable – their DNA does not allow them – to have both in their lives. And you know what? They are absolutely right! We cannot do this on our own. But if Christ's Spirit lives in us and empowers us and guides us then we absolutely can live this way.

When we act and live out one without the other, we are out of balance. And being out of balance has consequences. When you speak and act truthfully without grace involved, that is called self-righteousness. You are not giving the other person any grace; you are giving what truth alone would rightfully give them (and in your mind, rightfully so!). What you are really doing is viewing yourself as a judge – as morally and relationally superior - and immediately passing judgement on them. If God dealt with us this way, none of us would survive one more second. Truth without grace shows itself when humility has disappeared, and self-righteousness has taken over. This situation normally comes across as arrogant, haughty, angry, and prideful.

On the other hand, when you act graciously without truth, you are basically informing the person that you believe there are no boundaries, no reality, and they can live as they please – and you will approve. The subtle problem is that intentions are usually good when we act in grace without truth. Many times, we are trying to be kind to someone. But unfortunately, what appears nice on the surface is sinister underneath. Grace without truth leads to destruction of relationships and people. The parent who is not willing to give the child truth and training, and instead opts for overwhelming amounts of grace, ends up creating an adult-sized baby in many cases. The spouse who is not willing to share their true feelings about their relationship with their partner, in order to maintain some semblance of harmony, creates a chasm between them in the end. Grace with no truth is no good. If God dealt with us this way, He would tell us that we will *probably* be okay and make it to Heaven - even if we don't trust in Christ. This "grace" without truth would be deceitful – and lead to our destruction.

But praise God that was not His plan. The death, burial, and resurrection of Jesus Christ embodies both grace and truth for us – our sin debt is paid, and we didn't have to pay for it! The Bible says Jesus is full of grace and truth. It means that first of all, He is full of the grace of God that seeks the good of everyone – lost people included. This grace and love flow out of His inmost being – and the result is the cross of Christ. In order to bring about God's *gracious* plan of redemption - Jesus proclaimed the *Truth* of God in word and deed with absolute accuracy and perfection. In the phrase "*full* of grace and truth" the *and* is also significant. It means that there is a paradoxical, perfect blend of the two found in Jesus Christ. He is the only One Who can define reality this way. And He is the only Person Who can help you and I live our lives full of both grace and truth.

My observation is that most of us struggle with living out one or the other. We are usually very good at one, but not both. And most of the time we struggle in the same area consistently. Some people are very kind and gracious and merciful – they are peacemakers – and they have a hard time giving people the truth that needs to be shared. On the other hand, some people are *very* truthful all the time

– they will tell you exactly what they think! But they often do it with very little grace and love.

If you struggle showing people grace, make that a matter of prayer and remind yourself this way: take a piece of paper and write the word GRACE on it, and put it somewhere you will see it. Every time you see it, remember to pray and ask God to help you to have it. If you struggle with being truthful, write the word TRUTH on it, and put it somewhere you will see it. Every time you see it, remember to pray and ask God to help you to live truth in your words and actions.

The constant tension for us this side of glorification, is to find and maintain this paradoxical blend of grace and truth – and find blessings as we do so. Balance.

Small Group Discussion Guide

After reading the chapter discuss the following questions below.

1) Pilate asked Jesus the question "What is truth?".
How would YOU answer that question?

2) Read John 14:6 and John 17:17.
How does the Bible define truth?

3) Read Proverbs 3:3 and discuss:
What are we told to do with mercy (grace) and truth?
What is the promise for us if we do this?

4) Discuss the idea of balance in grace and truth:
What happens if we have a lot of truth but <u>no grace</u> in our life?
What happens if we have a lot of grace but <u>no truth</u> in our life?
What does it mean that Jesus is "full of grace and truth"?

5) Which area do you need the most help with in your life?
Grace or truth?

Bibliography

Cloud, Henry. *Boundaries for Leaders*. Harper Collins, 2013.

Cloud, Henry. *Boundaries in Marriage*. Zondervan, 2009.

Meyer, Jason. Lloyd-Jones on the Christian Life. Wheaton, IL: Crossway, 2018.

Morris, Henry. "The Bible, Creation, and Ecology." *Acts & Facts* (November 1991).

Pentecost, J. Dwight. "Daniel," in *The Bible Knowledge Commentary: An Exposition of the Scriptures*, ed. J. F. Walvoord and R. B. Zuck, vol. 1 Wheaton, IL: Victor Books, 1985.

The British Psychology Society Research Digest. Christian Jarrett. Infants Show a Preference for Toys That Match Their Gender Before They Know What Gender Is. Accessed: January 25, 2021. https://digest.bps.org.uk/2016/06/03/infants-show-a-preference-for-toys-that-match-their-gender-before-they-know-what-gender-is/

Wells, David. *God in the Wasteland: The Reality of Truth in a World of Fading Dreams.* Wm. B. Eerdmans Publishing, 1994.

Wiersbe, Warren. *Bible Exposition Commentary*. Wheaton, IL: Victor Books, 1996.

Wikipedia. "Restrictor Plate". Accessed: January 20, 2021. https://en.wikipedia.org/wiki/Restrictor_plate

Wikipedia. "Self-Concept". Accessed: January 26, 2021. https://en.wikipedia.org/wiki/Self-concept

ABOUT THE AUTHOR

Marc and Jessi Buxton are church planting missionaries in Metro Manila, Philippines. Their home church is the Florence Baptist Temple in Florence, SC. They have two sons, Reece and Levi, and a daughter, Nicole.

Marc is the founding pastor of Midpoint Baptist Fellowship in Marikina City, Philippines. He serves as the Provost & Senior Vice President of Global Life University (global-life.university). Marc is also the founder of Honest Deceiver Ministries, an evangelistic ministry that helps churches share the gospel through the art of illusion (honestdeceiver.com).

For more information on how you can support their growing ministry visit their website: **www.marcbuxton.com**

www.ingramcontent.com/pod-product-compliance
Lightning Source LLC
Chambersburg PA
CBHW030306130626
46549CB00002B/720